ROUTLEDGE LIBRARY EDITIONS:
EARLY WESTERN RESPONSES
TO SOVIET RUSSIA

Volume 14

A PHYSICIAN'S TOUR IN SOVIET RUSSIA

A PHYSICIAN'S TOUR IN SOVIET RUSSIA

SIR JAMES PURVES-STEWART

Routledge
Taylor & Francis Group
LONDON AND NEW YORK

First published in 1933 by George Allen & Unwin Ltd

This edition first published in 2018
by Routledge
2 Park Square, Milton Park, Abingdon, Oxon OX14 4RN

and by Routledge
711 Third Avenue, New York, NY 10017

Routledge is an imprint of the Taylor & Francis Group, an informa business

© 1933 James Purves-Stewart

All rights reserved. No part of this book may be reprinted or reproduced or utilised in any form or by any electronic, mechanical, or other means, now known or hereafter invented, including photocopying and recording, or in any information storage or retrieval system, without permission in writing from the publishers.

Trademark notice: Product or corporate names may be trademarks or registered trademarks, and are used only for identification and explanation without intent to infringe.

British Library Cataloguing in Publication Data
A catalogue record for this book is available from the British Library

ISBN: 978-1-138-04993-2 (Set)
ISBN: 978-1-315-11072-1 (Set) (ebk)
ISBN: 978-1-138-08298-4 (Volume 14) (hbk)
ISBN: 978-1-138-08365-3 (Volume 14) (pbk)
ISBN: 978-1-315-11219-0 (Volume 14) (ebk)

Publisher's Note
The publisher has gone to great lengths to ensure the quality of this reprint but points out that some imperfections in the original copies may be apparent.

Disclaimer
The publisher has made every effort to trace copyright holders and would welcome correspondence from those they have been unable to trace.

SEVEN EVILS—ONE ANSWER
On the flag: The Five-Year Plan in Four Years

A PHYSICIAN'S TOUR IN SOVIET RUSSIA

by

SIR JAMES PURVES-STEWART

K.C.M.G., C.B.

With reproductions of four Russian Cartoons

LONDON

GEORGE ALLEN & UNWIN LTD

MUSEUM STREET

FIRST PUBLISHED IN JANUARY 1933
SECOND IMPRESSION JULY 1933

All rights reserved

PRINTED IN GREAT BRITAIN BY
UNWIN BROTHERS LTD., WOKING

PREFACE

THE following notes were made by a practising physician from London during a month's visit to Russia in the summer of 1932. They make no claim to offer anything more than a transient view of the constantly changing conditions of Russian life. To those who knew Russia before the Great War, the present picture will be almost unrecognizable; what a future generation will think, cannot be foretold.

Seen as they are, through medical eyes, the salient points are bound to be different than had the observer been, say, an artist or a journalist; yet even to non-medical readers it is hoped they may perhaps be of interest.

CONTENTS

ILLUSTRATIONS

A PHYSICIAN'S TOUR IN SOVIET RUSSIA

CHAPTER I

COMMUNIST PROPAGANDA

ON BOARD M/V "DJERJINSKY"
OF THE SOVIET MERCHANT FLEET

August 14, 1932

All of us passengers were warned to be on board at Hay's Wharf, London Bridge, by 8 p.m. last night. Everything was well arranged: porters to carry one's baggage; guides to steer one to the correct cabin. A specially industrious sailor took great trouble in collecting my kit. I attempted to tip him. He refused, with great decision.

The service in the cabins is very smart. We went off to breakfast this morning, leaving our state-room in a chaotic mess. On our return, half an hour later, everything was spick and span.

This is a propagandist ship. The saloon is adorned with a portrait of the "hero" Djerjinsky, founder and arch-terrorist of the Tche-Ka during the Russian Revolution. The walls of the smoking-room are decorated with water-colours depicting revolutionist processions, all with red banners showing the

Soviet hammer and sickle. Even the ship's inkpots have this last device embossed on them, together with the red star of the U.S.S.R.

Up till the time when we left the dock-side, an enterprising newsagent on the middle deck did a brisk trade in communistic propaganda—magazines, newspapers, and novels.

We did not weigh anchor till 11.30 p.m., by which time my fellow-traveller and old friend, Dr. Frederick Green, M.C., was wisely asleep in his cabin. Everything is clean and tidy; the stewards prompt and polite. The whole of the first- and second-class accommodation is full up; the steerage has only about a dozen people.

This morning we held a meeting of the doctors' and scientists' party, to which we belong. This tour of ours has been organized by the S.C.R., or Society for Cultural Relations between the Peoples of the British Commonwealth and the U.S.S.R. At present we are fourteen in number, but another six or seven have gone in advance by an earlier ship and will join our party at Leningrad. We called the roll; each of us stood up in turn and was identified by the rest. We comprise amongst us physicians, surgeons, biologists, public health officials, teachers of biology, medical students, and a skilled engineer. We duly elected a chairman and a secretary.

This evening, after dinner, we attended an address by Lord M——y upon present economic conditions in Russia. Lord M——y is a Labour peer who is leading a party of his own to Russia. He has already been there himself. He is a clear and persuasive speaker and evidently an enthusiastic pro-Bolshevist.

According to his statements, the standard of living to-day in Russia is about 60 per cent above that of 1913 and is still rising. The average monthly wages of a Russian family are estimated at 150 roubles. Assuming the rouble at 3 shillings, the government exchange-rate,[1] this would be equivalent to £22 10s., or about 15 shillings a day. Necessities such as bread, milk, clothes, are rationed, both as to quantity and price, the official prices being very cheap. Rent is based on the government allotment of space, each person being entitled to 9 cubic metres, rented at 40 kopecks per cubic metre. If a worker receives a wage of 125 or 150 roubles a month, he pays a basic rent, amounting to not more than 10 per cent of his earnings. If his monthly wage exceeds 150 roubles, his rent for the same accommodation is correspondingly raised; thus for identical accommodation two adjacent families may pay different rents.

In addition, certain social services are provided free by the State, e.g. health insurance, widows' pensions (60 roubles per month) and old-age

[1] Subsequent inquiries in Russia give the basic monthly wages at about 120 roubles a month for a man and his wife. Moreover, the value of the rouble is entirely fictitious. For example, in Moscow, a few days later, I was able to buy roubles privately and without difficulty at 42 to the £, i.e. less than 6d. per rouble.

pensions, at the age of sixty years for men and fifty-five years for women. The amount of pension depends on the number of years worked, the maximum, viz. one-half of the wages, being attained after twenty years' work.

Each worker has two weeks' holiday a year, on full pay. If he is ill, he has free treatment and, if necessary, free travel to a sanatorium or home of recovery.

The prices of goods are on three levels:

1. Fixed prices for rationed necessities. These are low.

2. If the worker wishes to have more than his ration, he can supplement it by buying an extra quantity, but at a higher price.

3. "Open market" prices. These are very high. To some extent they are kept down by the "open co-operative" stores.

A difficulty is that with the rise in the standard of living the production of certain goods cannot keep pace with the demand, e.g. people who formerly did not buy boots now wish to have them.

The worker has an additional source of food-supply, viz. factory kitchens with communal dining-rooms under good hygienic conditions. Here the worker can buy a meal for 30 to 70 kopecks.

Ninety per cent of the population belong to "co-operative societies." These supply certain goods not obtainable as rations from government sources. The government provides capital for the development of these societies, which are sometimes actually in competition with the government factories.

The national income at present, according to Bolshevist statements, is being devoted mainly to capital development, to social services, and to workers' wages. The Russian worker is said to have more money than he actually needs(!). This excess income he spends on travel, scientific pamphlets, books, etc.

Russian loans are regularly over-subscribed, even loans which yield no interest. Market quotations of government loans without interest are just as high as those for loans yielding 9 or 10 per cent.[1]

Communism in Russia is almost a religion, although at present only 2 millions out of 160 millions are members of the Communist Party. Admission to the Party, for adults, requires a period of probation of two years, together with evidence of communistic activity. Adolescents are admissible after a probationary period of six months. No communist may receive a salary above 600 roubles monthly. If he makes more than this, he must hand over at least 20 per cent to the Party funds. In special cases, however, where a non-communist is receiving a larger salary for identical work, the communist's salary is pushed up, to prevent invidious comparisons.

Conditions in Russia are constantly changing,

[1] Are these really loans or compulsory levies? Every worker is "invited" to contribute three weeks' wages per annum to government loans.

every few weeks, corresponding to the varying communist decrees. Whether the ambition and outlook of individual workers are being swamped, Lord M——y does not know. He pointed out the scarcity of skilled workers and of scientists, but made no reference to one of the causes of the present scarcity of trained experts, viz. the indiscriminate massacre of such men during the Revolution. He was asked whether political liberty has or has not been extinguished under the Soviet system. To this he did not reply, but pointed out how columns of self-criticism by the workers fill the daily journals in Russia, such criticism being permitted by the government so long as the fundamental principles of socialism are not attacked. Illiteracy is claimed to be rapidly diminishing, from about 94 per cent before the War to about 15 per cent nowadays. Even old people are now learning to read and write.

As to the ultimate aims of the communist régime, the State must remain an organ of repression until class differences are wiped out. According to Karl Marx, "when the people become class-less, the State will wither away."

There is a special cabin in the crew's quarters set aside for propaganda and encouragement—a so-called "Lenin corner." This is a sort of chapel of the communistic creed. A small statuette of Lenin stands against one wall. Pictures of other communistic saints include photos of Marx, Liebknecht,

Engels, Rukoff, Kalinin, and Djerjinsky. Red banners are draped on all the walls, inscribed with slogans such as the following: "Under the leadership of the V.K.P.b.,[1] onward to the Triumph of Socialism"; "Hail to the power of Soviets throughout the World"; "Down with the Incendiary Intervention of War"; "Hail to the one and only Lenin Party and to the Comintern"; "Defend our Shores; strengthen our Transport."

Part of this "corner" is used as a dining-room, part for playing table games, such as chess, etc. The captain, a kindly soul with a benevolent Mongolian type of face, dressed in correct blue uniform with the usual gold stripes on his sleeves, looked in whilst I was there. He sat down beside the chess-players for a few minutes and watched the game. None of the crew stood up or paid any attention to him. The only other uniformed officer we have seen is the ship's doctor. None of the officers or crew speak English; a few of them talk German. They are all affable and willing to chat with the passengers. Some of the girl stewardesses are ardent propagandists. I asked one of them what her prospects would be twenty years hence. She thought she might perhaps, by that time, have a family of her own, but if not, she is sure she will be looked after, in some sort of institution for old people. Her present ambition is to travel about the world, and this she thinks will be possible by the aid of a

[1] All-united Communist Party, bolshevik.

Russian tourist agency, supplemented by a Government subsidy.

August 16th

Last night another meeting was held, under Lord M——y's chairmanship, to "discuss" the principles of communism. The discussion was one-sided. A preliminary description of Bolshevist political and military organization was given by our ardent communist chairman. The main points emphasized by him were as follows:

The U.S.S.R. is a federation of seven republics. Originally four in number, they have been supplemented by three more. They now include Russia proper (a federation of twenty-six smaller provinces), the Ukraine, White Russia, Trans-Caucasia (a federation of three provinces), Turkmenistan, Tajigistan, and Uzbekistan. Each of these republics, if it so desires, is free to break away from the U.S.S.R. At one time the Ukraine thought of seceding, but was "persuaded" not to do so.

The source of governmental power is the All-Union Congress of Soviets, which has about two thousand members, and meets every two years. Day-to-day work is carried on by a Union Council of two to four hundred members, which meets three times a year. In order that each of the seven constituent republics may have its views suitably represented, there is another chamber, the Council of Nationalities, meeting three times a year, to approve of legislation submitted to it from above.

The body which is constantly in session is the Presidium. This consists of twenty-seven members, nine from the All-Union Congress, nine from the Council of Nationalities, and nine selected from the two combined. The chairman of this Presidium, Kalinin, is the President of the Republic.

Voting for official positions in various government bodies is an indirect affair. Villages and town wards elect councils or soviets, one representative for every hundred votes. Voting is not by ballot, but by show of hands. Rural representatives are given only one-fifth the voting power of urban members, thereby assuring a preponderating influence to the urban population. The primary soviets elect representatives to a District Soviet. In turn the district soviets elect representatives to provincial, thence to regional, and these again to the All-Union Congress of Soviets.

Each government department, e.g. for education, public health, war, foreign affairs, etc., is presided over by a Commissar, or cabinet minister. The Council of People's Commissars has a chairman (at present Molotoff) corresponding to a prime minister. This Council of People's Commissars is the body which draws up or amends the laws, which are subsequently sent down for approval by the Council of Nationalities. Every member of the Council of People's Commissars is subject to removal by the Chief Commissar.

The Russian Army

Russians feel that they are surrounded by hostile nations. They recall how in 1920 Russia was invaded[1] by French, British, Italian, and Czecho-slovakian armies, all of which were beaten back. Subsequently for a time many foreign nations refused to establish diplomatic relations with Russia. England was the first to re-establish them, then came France, Italy, and others. The U.S.A. have not yet resumed diplomatic relations, although they have extensive trading relations through business firms. Poland, Rumania, and Japan are still profoundly antagonistic to Russia. This dislike shown towards her by foreign nations compels Russia to defend herself. The Red Army consists of 600,000 well-equipped men, under compulsory service, highly disciplined, "but not by methods of severity." She possesses good artillery, also a great air force, which is the pride of the army. Aeroplanes built in Russia are claimed to be better than the foreign models from which they are copied.

Russia does not want war; she wants to be left alone. She will never cross her own frontier to attack other nations, but will defend herself if Russian territory is invaded. Russia is in favour of universal disarmament, and actually proposed this to the League of Nations.

Sentries are posted at all factories, bridges, etc. This is in order to guard against counter-revolution.

[1] At the invitation of the anti-revolutionary Russian Party.

Every citizen, male or female, is taught to use arms. Russia feels that she is still in a state of war, against counter-revolutionaries at home, as well as against potential outside enemies.

What is the relation of the Communist Party to the government? As the various soviets rise in the scale of importance, the proportion of communists steadily rises, from about 50 per cent in the district soviets to 60 per cent in provincial soviets, 65 per cent in the regional soviets, 70 per cent in the All-Union Congress, and 80 to 90 per cent in the Council of People's Commissars, until we reach the Presidium of twenty-seven members, all of whom are communists.

The Council of Nationalities does not initiate laws; it considers legislation which has previously been formulated by the Presidium. Thus, in the end, the Communist Party is an autocratic organization, which controls the laws and administration of the whole country.

All decisions of a majority-vote of the Presidium must not only be accepted but also facilitated by the minority. Dissentient members who do not publicly express "repentance" are expelled from the Party, exiled to distant parts of the country, or "liquidated." No opposition to the views of the majority of the communist Presidium is tolerated. Hence the frequent "purges" whereby dangerous critics within the Party are got rid of (as in the case of Trotsky, the former Commissar for War).

The Communist Party admittedly fosters and finances subversive propaganda amongst the populations of foreign countries, e.g. in England.[1]

The lecturer was asked whether the Russian army is really a purely defensive organization as above described. He admitted that every communist, and every soldier in the Russian army, is expected to be a continuous and active propagandist.

The whole Press of Russia is owned and controlled by the Communist Party. No newspaper is free to criticize communist doctrines or to publish any anti-communist articles.

So far as I can make out, there are only four or five individuals in our passenger list of one hundred and twenty persons (outside our own little medical and scientific party of fourteen) who are not enthusiastic and vocal communists. The most eloquent of all are those who have not yet visited Russia. Communism is proclaimed by them to be the universal panacea for human unhappiness. Capitalist countries are those where there are employers and employed, or, in communistic language, "exploiters" (who make a profit from the labour of others) and "ex-

[1] Notwithstanding the clause in the Trade Agreements of 1921 and 1929: "To refrain and to restrain all persons and organizations under their direct or indirect control . . . from any act, overt or covert, liable in any way whatsoever to endanger the tranquillity or prosperity of any part or territory of the British Empire."

ploited" (who work for wages dealt out to them by their employers). To save and to invest money, even if it be the result of one's own labours, is to become a capitalist and an exploiter. To spend all one's wages is meritorious. The State will provide for the workers during sickness and old age.

This afternoon most of the crew, men and women, including the captain, collected on the after-deck to listen to an hour's lecture by one of the ship's engineers, on the subject of electrically driven motor-boats specially adapted for ice-breakers. Lectures of this sort, some of them technical, others propagandist, are part of the regular programme of the voyage. The lecturer had a blackboard on which he drew diagrams of a ship with Diesel engines charging the accumulators. He was bright and enthusiastic. The crew and captain listened with attention. At the end of the lecture several of the crew asked questions.

In the evening we had another communistic lecture, this time on the teachings of Karl Marx, by M., a young American Jew. His discourse was well thought-out and delivered, but somewhat side-tracked by its undue concentration on the effects of the present world slump on the U.S.A. His main points were as follows:

The new or communistic system of economics has been elaborated by Marx, who was the first to enunciate the idea of a "socialistic economic determinism," to determine the political and all other developments of the human race. Several basic contradictions are claimed by Marx to be inherent in the capitalist system. The first of these is the lack of balance between production and consumption. For example, in 1929 the total wealth of the U.S.A. was 400,000 million dollars; life insurances earned were about 100 millions; there were roughly 30 million families with 30 million automobiles. Prosperity seemed assured.

Since then has come the slump. Half of the industries in the U.S.A. have stopped production, and half the workers are out of work. Investments and savings have been largely wiped out. Why? Because when the total national income was 90 billion dollars the total income of workers and farmers amounted only to about 22 billions, i.e. less than 45 per cent of the national income. Surplus production has progressively increased, and yet each successive year has shown the rate of income received by the workers and farmers to be practically the same. The increasing accumulation of surplus goods could not be disposed of; hence factories were shut down. This further reduced the workers' income, and they became still less able to buy goods. Prior to 1929 a large proportion of goods, e.g. automobiles, radios, etc., were bought on the instalment plan. This has now come to an end. Moreover, the foreign markets which, prior to 1929, bought large quantities of goods, no longer do so to the same extent. The net result is that it is no longer possible for the U.S.A. to dispose of their accumulation of excess goods.

Even during the so-called boom time, between 1922 and 1929, the lecturer claims that there was no true prosperity in the U.S.A. except for the minority of people who possessed the means of production and distribution. During these boom years the average annual wages of workers were about 800 dollars, to support a family of four or five persons. This supposed prosperity, therefore, was an illusion.

The result has been the present economic depression, which, says the communist, can never end! The more factories that are closed, the less wages are earned, and the less surplus can be disposed of.

For this impasse capitalists have only the following solutions to offer:

1. To rationalize and reorganize industries; to reduce hours of labour, and to increase wages. But the capitalist still wishes to retain his same ratio of profit. But, so long as the workers only receive 45 per cent of the income, they can never buy 100 per cent of the products.

2. To start a new war on a large scale. Surplus labour will then be used for countries to fight each other. Meantime factories and other similar enterprises will have another boom.

The proper solution, according to the lecturer, is that of Karl Marx, viz. a "planned economy" which will organize industries and will control and co-ordinate production, not for profit, but to meet the needs of the people. The hours of labour will be adjusted to the efficiency of machinery. Wealth and income will also be so adjusted that the workers shall receive approximately 100 per cent of the income, deducting a certain proportion to be side-tracked for improvement of machinery, etc. Everyone will then be able to live in comfort. What will happen to the exploiters and the middlemen? "They will have to go to work."

Russia has already started to put these doctrines into operation. Since the Five-Year Plan of 1927 was set going, her national income is claimed to have risen from 10 to 32 billion dollars, i.e. 300 per cent; her mechanical and industrial output has increased four times; the efficiency of her mechanized workers has increased by 100 per cent, and it is prophesied that by the end of the second Five-Year Plan this efficiency will have increased to 500 per cent and will equal that of capitalistic countries.[1]

The Five-Year Plan has been devised specially to establish the heavy industries and to transform Russia from an agricultural into an industrial country. Light industries have been less urgently pressed forward, yet even in them the increase is

[1] This means that her efficiency was originally about one-tenth of the normal. This basic level, of course, is easier to improve upon than to increase an efficiency which was already at par.

claimed to have been about 180 per cent. Similarly with agricultural production(?).

Russia, therefore, in four years claims to have accomplished what it took England and the U.S.A. a hundred years to achieve. There has been a 500 per cent rise of production in Russia compared with a 30 per cent decrease in the U.S.A. On the other hand, in nations other than Russia during these same years all heavy industries have either remained stationary or, more often, have receded.

All this is claimed by the lecturer as the result of a "planned economy" in a crazy world.

The lecturer was asked as to how private wealth was to be got rid of and given back to the people "to whom it belongs." The answer was that the capitalist cannot be expected to give it up voluntarily; it must accordingly be taken from him either by taxation or by revolution. The capitalist will never yield up his wealth except by confiscation. Therefore the only practical way is by united decisive action of all the people. Capitalists themselves, he admitted, are less to blame than the capitalistic system. But the world cannot wait for the spontaneous collapse of capitalism.

He admitted that the high tariffs of the U.S.A. may have been a factor hindering the free exchange of goods, and thereby increasing the difficulties already inherent in the capitalistic system. It was also admitted that an economic depression in Europe preceded the American slump, and was precipitated by the War. International war debts are now hanging like a millstone round the necks of most European countries. The War undoubtedly precipitated the Russian Revolution and the advance of Russian communism. But the Revolution would have come in any case, within ten years or sooner.

Another speaker pointed out that it is one thing for peasants to seize land, which they can use themselves, but that in a highly industrialized country, if the workers were to seize trains, machinery, banks, etc., these could not be used by the workers themselves, because of the lack of skilled managers, directors, and experts. Nor could the workers, having seized the machinery and businesses, secure customers from abroad. The lecturer admitted that the real work of running complicated organizations is done by technical experts. These would be "taken over" by the workers,[1] whilst the boards of directors would be "eliminated." It was further pointed out to him that supposing the technical experts refuse to be "taken over," they cannot be improvised; consequently the complicated organizations will be wrecked and the workers will starve. The lecturer replied that it is better to have a quick and bloody revolution than starve slowly to death, waiting for a peaceful revolution. He compared revolution to a major surgical operation which may be necessary, e.g. by amputation of a limb, in order to save a patient's life. One of us

[1] At the same high salaries?

asked: "What if the patient dies under the operation?" To this there was no reply. It was further suggested to the lecturer that the patient, although he dies, will "die cured."

Communists in England say they cannot wait for a peaceful revolution. They foresee that, even if the Socialist Party secures a parliamentary majority to sanction the confiscation of capitalists' property, the capitalists will probably resist by force. Communists have no faith, therefore, in parliamentary or constitutional methods, remembering that England has already had two Labour Governments, neither of which has succeeded or attempted to overthrow capitalism, the capitalists in England having hitherto been able to sidetrack the class struggle which the communists desire to precipitate.

August 17th

In a conversation with a bright and fluent young Scottish communist, R., I tried to extract from him an explanation of the difference between a communist and a socialist, and also of the reasons why communists appear to be just as bitterly antagonistic to socialists as they are to capitalists, as evidenced by the frequent sanguinary fights in Germany between communists and socialists. His explanation seems to be that socialists, whilst supporting the ideal of abolition of capitalism, are willing to ally themselves with financiers, bankers, and other experts, trained under a capitalistic régime, and to co-operate with these experts for socialistic purposes. Socialists will tolerate a trained and efficient bureaucracy; communists, on the other hand, discard all idea of bureaucratic administration, even under socialistic government, and claim the right of the workers to dismiss or get rid of any expert, no matter how efficient or experienced, and to replace him at once by a loyal though inexperienced communist. Apparently every communist leader is considered capable of filling any expert government post.

Mr. R.-S., on the other hand, a Labour ex-M.P., a shrewd and logical thinker, whom I met to-day, is strongly antagonistic to the communist views. According to his definition, a worker is anyone who works with his hands or his brain, whereas the communistic definition of a worker seems to be that of an underpaid wage-slave. The socialist is against violent forceful revolutionary methods; he hopes to attain his ends by political means—evolution rather than revolution.

All this communistic propaganda has not been wasted on us, for it gives us a clearer idea of what to look out for, when we come to land on Russian soil.

CHAPTER II

LENINGRAD

August 18th

To-day we arrived at Leningrad. There are miles of busy wharves with stacks of pit-props and other timber; ships and barges being loaded and unloaded by gangs of men and women labourers; "Torgsin" stores (labelled in English, "universal shop"), where goods can be bought for foreign valuta, but not in Russian currency; scaffoldings for the erection of huge reinforced concrete sheds and warehouses. In the far distance we saw the golden cupola of the Isaaksky cathedral (now an anti-god museum), also the glittering golden spike of the Admiralty dome.

The broad quay-side at disembarkation was almost empty of foot passengers. We arrived at 2.45 p.m. and promptly left the ship, but were detained in the Custom-house until 5 p.m. The street traffic consisted of numerous trams, one private motor-car of English make (evidently provided for our communist peer), and one old droshky with a good horse, a shabby cab, and an ancient long-bearded isvostchik, clad in a flowing black blouse with a flat cap. He did not secure a fare. Several motor buses were awaiting our various parties, each of them draped along one side with a broad red streamer and a slogan: "Sport is one of the Necessities of the Five-Year Plan." A small crowd of plainly dressed people watched our ship from the quay. The young men and women were mostly bareheaded; the older men wore cloth caps and the women white kerchiefs.

We disembarked on to a floating barge which had an "underground" saloon for the sale of postage stamps, beer, cheap toys, and linen goods. The salesmen were slow but trustful; the customers helped themselves to drinks from one of the numerous bottles standing about, and paid afterwards. On the roofed-in deck of the Customs barge we waited patiently, a closely packed crowd of about one hundred and twenty. Each passenger's name was called out singly, making up successive batches of six, with about ten minutes' interval between each batch. Our particular group was not reached until all of the Lord M——y party had been got rid of.

In the Custom-house every article of baggage was opened. Apparently the only contraband discovered in our party was a couple of packs of playing-cards. These are a Government monopoly, and cannot be admitted, even by paying duty. The poor lady who owned them had therefore to give them up, in exchange for a receipt entitling her or her representative to reclaim them on re-embarking from Leningrad for a foreign port. Each of us had to declare the exact amount of foreign money in his possession. A written statement to that effect was provided, so that we shall not take out more foreign money than we bring in. We bought a little Russian currency, at the rate of seven roubles to the English pound.

At the Custom-house we were met by our official guide from the Intourist agency, an intelligent and sad-looking middle-aged lady. She skilfully shepherded us through the Customs, and on our exit presented us to three officials of the V.O.K.S. (*vsyo-susnye obshestvo kulturnaye svyoz*), i.e. United Society of Cultural Relations, who had kindly come to greet us. One of these, a sturdy and determined lady, was Mlle Wilm, vice-chairman of V.O.K.S.; another lady was Dr. Pelley, a medical representative of V.O.K.S.; the third was a gentleman, Dr. Miltin, representing the Public Health Department. These various officials accompanied us in our bus to the Octobraya Hotel, where they and our guide duly joined us at dinner. The bus was already partly occupied by our advance guard of six persons who had reached Leningrad a day earlier, and had been put up temporarily at an inferior hotel.

We drove off from the quay about 5 p.m. Soon we traversed the "Prospect of October 25th" (formerly the Nevsky Prospect, famed as the most brilliant street in Petrograd). This is a magnificent broad street with beautiful buildings, formerly hotels, banks, and *magasins de luxe*, but now transformed into workers' apartments on the upper floors, whilst the ground-floors are occupied by shabby little fruiterers, toyshops, ironmongers, barbers, beer-shops, and newspaper-shops. A few larger shops have been taken over by the Torgsin stores; these seem analogous but inferior to Woolworth stores in England and America. In many cases the shop sign is painted on an ill-fitting board above the door. Many shops are standing empty. Every beer-shop has its waiting queue of customers, forty or fifty or more, some carrying jugs, others with kettles, pans, or jars.

We had a fairly good dinner in the hotel restaurant, which must formerly have been a very smart place, judging by the remains of its original decorations. Even now it is clean and tidy, but rather like a Soho restaurant established in a Ritz building. The hotel itself has good parquet floors and staircases, but no carpets. F. G. and I have a suite with a private bathroom and lots of running water. The bath and wash-basin are devoid of plugs, but, having been forewarned in this respect, we had provided ourselves with the necessary accessories.

After dinner we were taken for a drive to see the "December Square" on the bank of the Neva. This square has the Senate and Synod on one side and the Admiralty on the other. In its centre stands an equestrian statue of Peter the Great. This was erected by Catherine under the guidance of Voltaire, who secured for her a French sculptor. The statue is not claimed to be a likeness of Peter, but shows him as an allegorical Roman emperor mounted on a spirited steed representing Russia. Under its hoofs is a large snake, emblematic of the forces of evil, being trampled underfoot. The Admiralty, now rather shabby, within its courtyard piled with old wooden rubbish, was originally constructed as a shipbuilding yard, with canals leading into the Neva. Later on these canals were filled in.

The Winter Palace Square, the largest in Leningrad, looks about four times the size of Trafalgar Square in London. On its north-west side stands the Winter Palace, together with the Hermitage Museum and Gallery of Art. This is the square where the tragedy of Bloody Sunday took place in 1905, when processions of workers, intending to present petitions to the Tsar, were shot down by his troops. Our guide enlarged on its horrors, relating how little boys, who had perched in the trees to see the fun, were shot down like birds by the first volley, aimed high over the heads of the dense crowds. After that date the Tsar no longer inhabited the Winter Palace. In 1917 it was occupied for a time by the Kerensky Provisional Government, but on October 25, 1917, the Soviet forces, in overwhelming strength, took possession, captured the Kerensky officials and sent them across the river to be imprisoned in the Peter and Paul fortress.

Opposite to our hotel, in the October Square, is the main railway station to Moscow. In the middle of the square is an enormous squat equestrian statue of Alexander III. Both the emperor and his steed have a huge gluteal development, almost of Epstein proportions, and the whole affair is so stodgy and grotesque that, even in Tsarist times, demands were made for its removal.

Later in the evening we were conducted to a park of amusement, formerly the private garden of one of the imperial palaces. This park was thronged with young Leningrad citizens and their young women. Bands, booths, and shooting-galleries were scattered about. There was a big open-air theatre, seating about two thousand people. Here we witnessed a variety show, comprising songs, dances, acrobatics, a one-act comedy, and a couple of back-chat humorists burlesquing the shortcomings of their respective co-operative societies. From this theatre we came away at half-time, and walked back to our hotel which, our guide assured us, was "just round the corner." It turned out to be a distance of a mile and a half.

Supper in the hotels goes on from midnight till about two in the morning. At one o'clock I strolled across the square to the Moscow railway station. This was positively jammed with miserable humanity, sitting and sleeping, on the platforms, in the waiting-halls, and even under the open archways in the rain and mud. These people were evidently workers, some of them well clad and wearing leather boots, others with straw tied around their feet, or even bare-legged. Queues numbering hundreds were waiting at the ticket-offices. Every train that came in was crammed to the doors. I don't envy those of our party who are due to travel "hard" in company with the workers. The whole scene was like a bank holiday in the East End of London, only much more sordid. This was not a special occasion of any sort, but owing to the overlapping of the five-day weeks in Russia every day is a holiday for one-fifth of the population—and yet these people did not look like holiday-makers either.

The people in the streets, mainly of a peasant type, are healthy looking, and plainly but comfortably dressed as a rule. A few aristocratic old men are conspicuous by the special shabbiness of their attire. One wonders whether they are survivors of the pre-war intelligentsia.

Leaving the main Prospect and strolling around the side streets, we saw the night life of some of the workers. In every doorway, and also on the pavements and on many islands in the open street, lay closely packed, filthily clothed men and women, and even a few children, without shoes or stockings, huddled together, asleep, not in scores but in hundreds—sometimes piled in pyramids, packed like a football scrum.

Workers' clubs, in ground-floor or underground rooms, seen through the open windows, were crowded with workers, smoking and drinking. From every club door drunken men were staggering out, whether leaving voluntarily or under pressure from their comrades it was difficult to say. Numerous prostitutes plied in the streets in the earlier part of the night. We did not venture inside a worker's club itself; it seemed prudent not to try.

I understand, from a communist Russian, that these poor down-and-out wretches are mostly "misfits," unemployable peasants who have migrated from the country to the city, but finding themselves unemployable, have sunk to poverty and rags. For a time the Government tried to detain them in special homes or institutions, in the hope of controlling their children if the parents were intractable; but the peasants always escaped. They constitute an impoverished and degraded class, relatively more numerous than in the slums of London or other great European cities.

August 19th

We drove out in a bus expedition to the suburbs, passing an old Lavra or monastery, now converted into workers' dwellings; also numerous factories taken over by the State, often with a large villa alongside, formerly the director's mansion, but now divided up into workers' apartments.

We visited a beautiful new prophylactorium, of which there are said to be twenty-five others of similar type in various parts of Leningrad alone. There is an institution of this sort in each district for the prevention and treatment of diseases in their early stages. It is a spacious new building, of which any modern city might well be proud. Like every public institution in Russia it is smothered, outside and in, by red banners with communistic slogans. Over the front entrance we read: "Those who work here must be on the highest level of the Socialistic Edifice." There is a large lecture-hall, with its inevitable bust of Lenin, draped in two red flags. The overhanging banner reads: "Shame to those who leave the Socialist Front, loafers and deserters!" "Long live Proletarian Discipline!" "Long live the V.K.P., organizer and leader of the Socialist Revolution!"

Each of the twenty-six prophylactoria in Leningrad corresponds to a local population of about 80,000 workers in a single district. The chief aim of the institution is the prevention of diseases; treatment, except of minor maladies and venereal diseases, is of secondary interest. There are special departments for tuberculosis, orthopaedics, children's ailments, ophthalmology, nose and throat diseases, etc. Each department has its own well-arranged consultation-room, treatment-room, and operating theatre. The waiting-rooms are hung with dramatic posters, illustrating the lurid results of different diseases, especially of venereal maladies, and the various modes in which they may be acquired. There are also posters illustrating the dangers of flies, the importance of cleanliness, etc. Each prophylactorium is in close association with all the factories in its neighbourhood. The social conditions of every worker and of his family are studied, recorded, and tabulated. Every worker, healthy or sick, is examined four or five times a year, and if signs of incipient or advanced disease are found, the patients are sent on to a prophylactorium or hospital as the case may be. In some special occupations a medical examination is made every month, e.g. barbers, workers in food and in dangerous trades, etc. The prophylactorium has no wards or beds, only the necessary operating-rooms for a polyclinic clientèle. There are complete X-ray, orthopaedic, light and heat, hydrotherapeutic and physico-therapeutic departments, each under its own specialist. The medical staff consists of about one hundred and twenty doctors, mostly young women. There are large, well-equipped chemical and histological laboratories, but with very few workers in them. On the wall of one of these laboratories hangs the usual red banner, inscribed this time with a sentiment attributed to Claude Bernard: "Do not be afraid of Contradictions; they lead us forwards." Venereal patients are carefully examined and treated at least once a month. If the patient fails to turn up, a warning notice is posted to him; thus a careful follow-up of each case and of his family is carried on. Venereal diseases, so we are told, are rapidly diminishing in Russia. This is attributed to three chief reasons: the absence of prostitution, the advance of education, and the systematic instruction of citizens in contraceptive methods.

We crossed the Neva to the far side of Leningrad, passing the Finland railway station. Here stands a spirited bronze statue of Lenin, in an oratorical attitude, erected on the exact spot where he addressed the workers on his famous arrival from Finland, accompanied by his colleague Trotsky. No reference or memorial is raised to Trotsky.

The Metchnikoff Hospital, so named in memory of the famous French bacteriologist who died about 1916, is a pre-war institution with accommodation at present for 2,000 patients. It consists of a series of large three-storey pavilions, built within a large park. Each pavilion has about 180 beds, but additional pavilions are being added to bring up the total to three thousand beds. Eminent physicians, surgeons, and specialists are on the staff. The director is a non-medical man. The most famous of the surgeons, Feodoroff, lives in the institute. We were conducted round the cancer pavilion, under the charge of Professor Petroff. In addition to well-lighted and spacious wards of various sizes, accommodating from one to twenty patients, there are operating-rooms, laboratories, X-ray and radium departments, and a good popular cancer museum of specimens, casts, and photographs. These are incongruously interspersed with the usual communistic slogans on the inevitable red banners, e.g.: "Through Co-operation and Mechanization we shall lead the country to Socialism." There is a good nursing staff, with one trained nurse to every eight beds in general medical wards, one to every six beds in gynaecological and surgical wards, and one to every four beds in cancer wards. The patients get up, or are wakened for tea, at 8 a.m.; the physicians and surgeons begin work at 9 a.m.

Several cancer patients under radium treatment for cancer of the lip, tongue, or throat, were shown to us. We also saw the special installation for deep X-ray therapy of uterine cancer, and were given encouraging accounts of its value in curing early cases, in mobilizing previously fixed tumours so as to render them operable, and in prolonging life in inoperable cases.

The Metchnikoff Hospital has its own huge electric power plant, independent of the city supply; also a large fruit and vegetable farm, which renders it self-supporting as regards agricultural products, except for potatoes. Pigs and cows are also raised on the hospital farm.

After so-called midday lunch at 4 p.m., a later trip took us to see other public buildings and monuments, all of them supposed to convey some communistic lesson, carefully emphasized by our sad-faced guide.

The former Champ de Mars, where whole battalions could be paraded and drilled, is now laid out as a public garden, named the "Square of the Martyrs of the Revolution." Here some two hundred of the revolutionaries of 1917 are buried in a common grave, marked by a huge granite terrace with poetic inscriptions. Several outstanding leaders are buried in separate graves within this square memorial. One or two leaders, who have died peacefully since those militant days, also lie here—a sort of Valhalla for communist heroes.

At one end of the "Bridge of Equality" (formerly the Troietsky Bridge) is a large white building fronting on the Neva. This was formerly occupied by the English Embassy, and is now a school. From the balcony of the Embassy in 1917 the British Ambassador, Sir George Buchanan, used to address the Russian citizens, exhorting them to stick to their allies and to pursue the war to a victorious end. At the other end of this same bridge is a building with a projecting stone balcony from which Lenin used to harangue the same crowd, urging them to make peace with Germany. Just beyond this is a beautiful Mohammedan mosque with a blue-tiled dome and two slender stone minarets. It has a magnificent blue-tiled sunken doorway, indented with smaller recesses. Every Friday a Mohammedan service is still held here; the remaining six days of the week being reserved for anti-religious propaganda.

Driving across a subsidiary branch of the Neva, spanned by a wooden bridge, from which the body of the slaughtered Rasputin was flung through the ice in 1916, we drove to an island dotted with beautiful villas, formerly the residences of wealthy merchants. All of these, nearly forty in number, are now occupied as "homes of rest" for weary workers who desire two weeks' holiday. The house we inspected was formerly the private mansion of a rubber magnate. It now houses one hundred workers. The large dining-room, salon, and other public rooms still contain pre-war statuary, bronzes, paintings, gilded candelabra, and carved mantel-pieces, all somewhat florid and Teutonic in style. Long wooden tables with cheap bent-wood chairs were laid out in preparation for the next meal. The former drawing-room was furnished as a dormitory with iron beds.

We crossed the Neva once more, driving along streets being cleaned by women sweepers, to visit the magnificent Uritsky Palace, formerly the Potemkin Palace, built in the eighteenth century by Prince Potemkin, the conqueror of the Crimea. From 1906 to 1917 this was the seat of the Russian Duma, and during 1917 the centre of political life in Russia. It is at present occupied by the Communistic State University. After the defeat of the Kerensky Provisional Government in 1917, Kerensky with his colleagues moved over the river to the Winter Palace, from which they were forcibly evicted and imprisoned on the famous October 25, 1917. A magnificent domed hall with gigantic pillars leads to an inner pillared hall. Here at one time Kerensky at one end of the hall addressed the throng as "ladies and gentlemen," the middle platform speaker called them "citizens," whilst Lenin at the other end addressed the same crowd as "workers." Beyond this great hall is the large amphitheatre, or Assembly Hall, formerly occupied by the Duma. This is now adorned with a gigantic black-and-white cartoon of Stalin, whilst a statue of Lenin is in the centre, and the stereotyped red banners and slogans are affixed all round the hall above the cornices.

Lastly we visited the Smolny Convent, the aristocratic school founded by Catherine II for daughters of the nobility. These girls were separated from their parents for seven or eight years, during which they never left the convent grounds, thus training a select species of humanity from which ladies-in-waiting for the Imperial Court were chosen. In front of the main entrance to this enormous building is a bronze statue of Lenin. In the main angle of the façade the Imperial arms are now replaced by the communistic sickle and hammer. Two arched porticos have been erected in front of the main building. One of them is inscribed "Workers of the World, Unite!" and the other, "The First Soviet of the Proletarian Dictatorship." The convent is now occupied by the soviets of the Leningrad province, together with various other Governmental committees and officials. We entered the Soviet Chamber without let or hindrance and watched a Russian orator haranguing the company from a rostrum, projecting like a pulpit in front of the main platform occupied by the chairman and several colleagues. A beautifully dressed young woman with well-displayed limbs sat below the rostrum, apparently the official stenographer.

Finally we were shown over the small suite, of two rooms, occupied by Lenin and his wife for several months. The inner room is furnished with Spartan simplicity. Its original furniture—a sofa, a couple of easy-chairs, a writing-table, and a cheap cabinet against the wall—is still here. The far end of the room is partially fenced off by a wooden partition to hold two iron beds, a plain built-in cupboard, and a huge Russian tiled stove in the corner.

The walls of the outer room, where Lenin received his visitors in audience, are covered with red-margined photos and specimens of contemporary revolutionary numbers of *Pravda* and other newspapers, giving the original diary of the historic October 25th–26th, almost hour by hour, culminating in the storming of the Winter Palace at 2 a.m. in time to be announced at a special night-sitting of the Congress of Soviets in the Smolny building.

Our guide then treated us to a short lecture on the virtues of Lenin, his passion for Beethoven's music (which he had to give up lest his heart became too tender), his devotion to little children, on whose heads he would lay his kindly hands (reminding one of a greater leader in Palestine 1,900 years earlier). All this, in view of the subsequent horrible atrocities at which he connived, and many of which he instigated, was somewhat nauseating. But our guide recited it faithfully to the end.

August 20th

I had a little chat with our lady guide about the present economic conditions of life in Russia. Everybody, whatever his or her income, pays an annual tax of 1 per cent. In addition, he pays one-tenth of his wages for lodging, including water-supply. Also subscriptions to his trade-union and to the Soviet Red Cross. He has his food card, entitling him to buy his rations of food, clothing, etc., at "government prices." Any excess of necessities or luxuries he pays out of his own pocket. Savings are not encouraged, although 7 per cent government loans are occasionally issued, to which workers are "invited" to subscribe. These shares cannot be sold without permission from a government committee. The total deductions from his wages amount to at least one-fourth of his income. It is no longer possible to bequeath property by will. Wills do not exist. When a citizen dies, his goods revert to the State. A local committee can either sell these and turn over the proceeds to the government or it can allow the citizen's children to buy them at a reduced rate.

Marriage is a peculiar institution, consisting in

D

being "registered." The only advantages of being married are that in case of subsequent divorce the joint property is divided equally between the two parties, also that before being registered both parties must produce medical certificates of freedom from venereal disease and from active tuberculosis. Consequently about half of the workers live in "free unions" without being "registered." The child of a free-union pair has no disability as compared with the child of "registered" parents. A child can assume the surname of either his father or his mother at will. As a matter of custom, he usually takes his father's surname. If a registered couple divorce, and there is a child still under age, the child is usually given into the mother's custody and the father pays 30 per cent of his wages for the child's upkeep. If there is more than one child the father pays up to 50 per cent of his wages, not more. Three divorces is the maximum number allowed to the ordinary individual; any extra marriage and divorce above that number must be by special Government consent.

We saw a worker's funeral in the street to-day, a pink coffin with wreaths of red flowers on top, loaded on a simple little open hearse, drawn by one horse and followed by a small crowd of mourners in working clothes. No religious ceremony takes place at a communistic funeral, only a farewell speech at the graveside and, if the deceased worker has been prominent, a band to play communist songs. There is, however, no official objection to a citizen being buried by a priest after a religious ceremony in church, if the friends so desire. Christian coffins are usually black; communist coffins white, red, or yellow.

We drove out, over incredibly rough cobbled suburban roads, to a wonderful Institute for Mother and Child, standing in its own grounds. This has seven hundred and fifty beds; five hundred of them are for diseased women and children; the other two hundred and fifty are for the observation and treatment of healthy mothers and children. A good many of the healthy children are foundlings, orphans, or children who have lost one parent. These orphans are kept in the Institute until the age of four years, when they are handed over to the Committee of Education to be brought up in kindergartens, and later in schools.

All maternity patients in the district are delivered in hospital; no mother bears a child at home, except by accident. The maternal deaths in labour work out at only 0·15 per cent. That is exclusive of eclampsia cases, in which the death-rate is 7 per cent, in spite of (subcutaneous $MgSO_4$) treatment. The proportion of eclamptic cases is 2 per cent, and is rising somewhat. Out of the last two thousand deliveries there were only 1·2 per cent of septic cases; six cases per thousand required forceps.

We were shown over a maternity ward by the chief surgeon, an elderly woman. All the women patients were in various stages of labour; a few were crying out. No anaesthetics are used, except in complicated cases.

The infants after birth are stacked in rows of little cots, twenty-eight in a ward. Each infant is carefully labelled with a serial number, one on a card at the head of the bed, another stamped on a piece of gauze wrapped round its wrist, and another in indelible pencil marked on its trunk. No case is known in which one infant has been confused or changed for another.

The principles of maternity are taught to girls as part of their school education. Contraceptive instruction is only given to those who have had a child. Abortions are performed for any women who so desire, according to one doctor's statement no charge being made; according to another, a fee of 25 roubles being taken.

Normal children, from infancy up to the age of three or four years, are kept in nurseries or in outdoor gardens and playgrounds, carefully nursed, fed, and trained. By the age of eighteen months to two years the average child can already wash and dress itself. Special little wooden steps lead the little tots up to the level of the wash-basins. In the children's play-room, full of "useful" toys, such as boats, spades, etc., and furnished with large mirrors, there is the usual Lenin bust with red flags and banners. The slogan here was, "Like bees, we learn to work, although we like to play." This is in a play-room for children under three years, who have not yet learned to read. On the wall of the entrance to this block is a diagram showing the incidence of various diseases in the building for the six years since its commencement, 1925 to 1930 inclusive: measles, two cases, both in 1926; scarlet fever, five cases, all in 1926; diphtheria, four cases, all in 1929; whooping-cough, no cases. Only two children died, both in 1929, apparently from diphtheria.

Amongst sick children the mortality is said to be 14 per cent under the age of a year, of whom 7·1 per cent die at birth. In pre-revolutionary days the mortality under twelve months of age was stated to be 44 per cent.

After seeing the children being fed and nursed, also others playing in the grounds, we were taken through the infants' kitchen. Here infants' diets are prepared and issued, not only to the infants still in hospital, but also to those up to the age of eighteen months who have been taken home by their mothers, who call daily for the twenty-four hours' supply of food, for which they pay 1 to 1½ roubles daily. The mother takes the child to the factory crèche when she goes to work, and takes it home after finishing work in the evening. In the institutional kitchen food bottles and food jars are carefully cleaned and sterilized. Milk is sterilized by exposure to 100° C. for five minutes, which is said not to destroy its vitamins. For sick children special diets (e.g. mixtures of egg, milk, and meat juice) are made up. A special flavoured mixture called Kisél is often sent out, containing fruit-juice, sugar, and potato flour.

All these health institutions are lavishly equipped and staffed. The Government is said to spend about 13 per cent of the total national income on health services and about 25 per cent on education.

We visited the Balinski mental hospital, a pre-revolutionary, rather shabby building, designed for 100 private patients and now holding 235, the majority being men. There are eleven medical officers. Only acute cases are admitted, chronic and demented patients being treated elsewhere. Most of the patients are schizophrenics, some of whom, especially those with excessive growth of hair along the back of the trunk, are treated by adrenalin injections daily for forty or fifty days, on the theory that the disease is due to endocrine deficiency. In other cases of schizophrenia abscess-therapy is used. Cases of dementia paralytica, thirty-three in number at present, are treated by malaria, followed, after twelve febrile "spikes," by a course of 3 grams of neo-salvarsan. Excited patients, as usual, are kept in warm baths for five or six hours daily. The garden and exercise-grounds are grubby and depressing. I inquired as to the mode of admission to a mental hospital. A single certificate by a district psychiatrist is enough to admit a patient, who is not seen by any layman before admission. If the friends so desire, they can take the patient out of hospital, or he can leave voluntarily if he can be kept under observation at his own home. I saw one schizophrenic man-patient, a severe case of katatonia, leaving the hospital in charge of a young woman.

The chief psychiatrist informs me that, since the revolution, traumatic "compensation" psychoses no longer occur—a highly significant fact, worthy of note in capitalist countries. The only traumatic psychoses still remaining are those following war injuries.

A night sanatorium, one of the four in Leningrad, was an interesting affair. Housed in the confiscated villa of a German sugar magnate, it still possesses opulent bronze doors and staircases, gilded candelabra and elaborate mahogany fittings, all now somewhat dingy, together with a number of huge oil paintings and some good statuary. The gardens, with their avenues of trees, fish-ponds, and arched summer-houses, planned to form a vista, are now rank and neglected.

This night sanatorium, which accommodates 125 persons, is for early cases of tuberculosis in workers who work in factories in the daytime and come here in the afternoons, between 4.30 and 5.30, to stay the night. A batch of men comes in for five weeks, then a five weeks' batch of women, and so on. Patients are eligible for readmission later on. Each day on admission the workers have a warm shower-bath and change into hospital khaki uniform. We saw them sitting down to an excellent evening meal, at which the conversation, strictly forbidden by placards on the walls, was loud and cheery. (No living power can muzzle the natural eloquence of the Russian man; what the achievements of the female may be, I cannot venture to guess.) After supper the inmates rest for an hour, play games from 8 till 10.30, and then turn in to sleep in the magnificent salons, neatly laid out with rows of tidy iron beds, placed considerably closer together than our English tuberculosis experts would have allowed. A temperature-chart for each patient is kept: if the evening figure is above $37{\cdot}3°$ he is transferred for whole-time treatment to a sanatorium or hospital. The worker goes back to his work in his factory each morning. Every patient's sputum is examined, and is said to be positive in about 4 or 5 per cent of cases. Such patients are grouped in a ward apart from the others, but are not provided with sputum flasks to take with them to their factory in the day. The medical director claims no cures by these five weeks' courses, but believes that the rest, régime, etc., do the patients good. To the outside observer it seems doubtful whether much permanent benefit is likely to be attained by the withdrawal of a patient from his family for so short an interval. But the evident desire to help the tuberculous patient is praiseworthy.

The Institute for Study of Dietectics is a new

organization which has been going on for less than two years. It is housed in a magnificent villa, built by the late Tsar Nicholas II in 1906 for the ballerina Kshesinskaya at a cost of about 2 million roubles. The director, Dr. Kolsobe, addressed us exhaustively for an hour on the work of the Institute, which studies dietetics in healthy and diseased workers—the quality of different foods and optimum methods of preparation, the planning of economic diets, the construction of kitchen stoves and utensils, the optimum diet for workers at various ages and in various occupations, also the instruction of skilled communal cooks, of whom there is at present a shortage. There are culinary experimental laboratories (kitchens) attended by cookery students. Here various methods are being tried out, e.g. plans whereby peeled potatoes may remain white instead of undergoing discoloration. Healthy "workers" come to the experimental dining-rooms, where different diets are served out to them at nice little tables. Some of them then have their gastric contents removed and analysed. We were shown a neat little endo-gastric camera for taking photographs of the gastric mucosa. The stomach is carefully washed out and filled with air; then the tiny camera with a dozen objectives, the whole not larger than a plum stone, is lowered into the stomach at the end of a stomach-tube, carrying the wire which induces an instantaneous flashlight when desired. We saw various laboratories, all well-equipped, and met some of the workers, men and women. A light supper of Bulgarian milk, ices, cream cakes, and tarts was then given us. Here we were joined by various Russian medical colleagues, some of whom had met us already at other medical institutions. I sat next to Dr. Shapiro, a man of forty-eight, professor of uro-genital surgery at the Metchnikoff Hospital. He proclaims himself an enthusiastic communist. He has two sons, one an officer in the Red Army, the other an engineer. He professes to have no regrets at being reduced in wages to a fraction of what he earned in pre-revolutionary days. Last winter he was sent to organize hospital work in the labour colonies in the north, where the conditions, he said, were appalling. He managed to get a hospital erected, and a doctor from the Metchnikoff Hospital was then sent out to run it.

He sang paeans of praise about the communistic régime and how he revelled in helping his fellow-citizens. He admitted, however, that although thinking is "free," and everybody ought to think communistically, it is not always wise to put one's thoughts into words. Another Russian colleague said: "If you think, don't speak; if you speak, don't write; if you write, don't publish."

August 21st

F. G. and myself attended a religious service in the large Znamenskaya Church close to our hotel.

It is a large, richly decorated building with side chapels, beautiful marble pillars, sacred pictures, numerous gold ornaments and ikons. There were no signs of pillaging. An impressive Russian service was going on, with priests in richly embroidered vestments and a mixed choir of men and women, not in vestments, with glorious Russian voices.

The church porch was full of beggar women. The crowded congregation was made up mostly of shabbily dressed, middle aged and elderly men and women, a few young people, and still fewer children. Devout worshippers not only crossed themselves, but knelt and touched the stone floor with their foreheads. Small tapers were sold to worshippers. One of the saleswomen wore a brooch with a hammer-and-sickle ornament. The priests were typical bearded Russians, one of them with a haunting, hollow-eyed face.

At the river frontage of the gardens of the Winter Palace the huge bronze gates are in process of demolition, as the gardens are now thrown open as a public park.

The FORTRESS OF PETER AND PAUL occupies an island on the Neva. Access is obtained by a wooden bridge. The old stone bastions and fortifications surround a central square some little distance in, with an avenue of trees leading up to it.

This island, captured from Sweden in 1703 by

Peter the Great, was intended by him to be the centre of his future capital. On one side of the central square is the Mint, which has struck all Russian coinages ever since, and recently carried out an issue of coinage for Persia.

Opposite the Mint is the Cathedral of SS. Peter and Paul, finished about 1720. It is a domed building with a curious tall needle-like gilt spire. Inside are the tombs of the Tsars and Tsaritzas from Peter onwards. All these are of white marble, each inscribed with the monarch's name, with gilded bronze eagles at the corners, and a gilt cross on the top slab. Two exceptions are the green jasper tomb of Alexander II, who abolished serfdom, and the pink quartz monument of his wife. There are also a few other tombs of archdukes and princes of royal blood. Prior to the revolution, this church was extraordinarily richly decorated. Its floor was carpeted and its walls, now bare, were hidden by hundreds of golden and silver wreaths. These were sold in 1919 by the Government to provide food for famished peasants in the Volga who were dying in thousands, and some of whom had been driven to cannibalism.

The Dutch clock in the clock tower of the cathedral used to chime the quarters, and at each hour played "God Save the Tsar." It has recently been remodelled so as to play the communist "International". At present, however, it is stuck at 11.56, so we did not hear it.

The earth on which the cathedral is built was

carried by hand by the Russian serfs on to the swampy island. Many of them died from privation and were buried close by, so that in the following century when further buildings were erected they were noised abroad as built "on the bones of the people."

In early days only the Tsar and his entourage had the right of entry to the cathedral, except on occasions of funerals, when delegations were admitted to the ceremony. The Tsar's canopied stall still exists, across the aisle directly opposite the pulpit, a most unusual position in a Greek Orthodox church.

The casement cells of SS. Peter and Paul have always been reserved for political prisoners—a sort of Russian Bastille. Confinement in such a casement meant imprisonment for life. No one is ever known to have escaped. The number of cells is seventy-two, arranged in two floors of thirty-six. All the cells are gloomy, whilst from the basement cells one cannot even glimpse the sky. The December revolutionary leaders were incarcerated here in 1825, and five of them were hanged in chains on the outer bastions. Prisoners were blindfolded during their journey to the prison; on arrival their own clothes were replaced by prison uniform, and a number was assigned to each instead of a name. Absolute silence prevailed, even in the corridors, which were carpeted with matting, so that the prisoners might not hear the warders walking along to inspect them through a horizontal slit in the door. Food was passed in through a small wicket-opening in the massive oaken door. No prisoner ever saw another prisoner. When the number of prisoners was only about fifteen, each was allowed out for half an hour's daily exercise in an inner courtyard in charge of two gendarmes. When the cells were full, exercise was allowed only every two or three days. There is a bath-house where a prisoner could have a bath, once in two months, always alone.

We were shown the cell where Prince Kropotkin was confined from 1874 to 1876 on account of his educationist propaganda. Being of noble blood, he was allowed special privileges, and here he completed his book on geography. He was only allowed to write up till sunset. He kept himself in good physical training by walking seven miles a day in his cell, estimating the distance by picking up a cigarette from one corner and, after walking round the room, laying it down in another. Kropotkin, after a couple of years, became so ill that he was transferred to the hospital of another military prison. From this he escaped and reached England. His brother in Russia was then arrested and sent to Siberia, where after one-and-a-half years he committed suicide.

A revolutionary girl-student, Vera Figner, was confined here in 1881 for a year, and subsequently in the political prison at Schlüsselberg, from which she was released in 1905 after twenty-four years' imprisonment. She is still alive in Moscow, a very old woman.

In spite of the silence, or rather because of it, the prisoners managed to communicate with each other by tapping on the wall, according to a code alphabet arranged in six rows, as follows:

	1	2	3	4	5
I	А	Б	В	Г	Д
II	Е	Ж	І	Й	К
III	Л	М	Н	О	П
IV	Р	С	Т	У	Ф
V	Х	Ц	Ч	Ш	Щ
VI	Ъ	Ю	Я		

To use this code, two sets of taps were given on the wall. The first set of taps gave the number of the vertical row, the second the number of the letter in that vertical row; e.g. to tap the letter K, this would be two taps and then five, and so on.

A similar code of communication is in existence amongst prison convicts in other countries, England included.

One woman prisoner, Maria Vietróva, whose cell we saw in the basement, successfully burnt herself to death by setting fire to the kerosene from her oil-lamp. Since then illumination, first by gas and subsequently by electric bulb, has been provided from behind a small circular plate of thick unbreakable glass. The table and bed, and in some cases even the stool, are riveted into the floor, to prevent a desperate prisoner from injuring himself, e.g. by lying on the floor and thrusting a leg of the iron bedstead down his throat.

The black punishment cell in the basement has its windows completely occluded by an iron shutter in the right-hand lower corner, of which a small flap can be locked or unlocked to give a feeble glimmer of light. Here refractory prisoners were confined two, three, or even five days at a time. Shapoválоff, a friend of Lenin, was confined here towards the end of the nineteenth century.

The last time these cells were used for prisoners was in 1921, during an attempted counter-revolution. Since 1922 they have been a museum. Several cells are fitted out with wax models of prisoners, one sitting at a table, another looking upwards to his barred window, and so on.

On the way back we saw across the river the former Bourse, with its blue and white façade on the river front. This is now used as a hall for exhibitions or public meetings.

The former military barracks are now the central offices of the electric supply department—"Electrotok."

The Hermitage is a fine building with a pillared portico supported by enormous muscled figures about 24 feet high, on whose bowed shoulders rest the transverse beams. Niches in the main wall of the building contain bronze statues of distinguished men, including Mark Antony, Raphael Mirglu (broken off above the ankles), Winkelmann, etc.

The picture-gallery and museum are said to be surpassed only by two others in the world, viz. the Louvre in Paris and the National Gallery in London. We were rapidly conducted through magnificent galleries with masterpieces of painting and sculpture, including Michael Angelo's granite figure of a squatting boy, fashioned from a small cubic mass of rock; also Titians, Giorgiones, Caravaggios, Rembrandts, Hals, etc. The Russian guides who lead the workers round are careful to draw communistic lessons from all the various schools of art, pointing out how these works were executed for the hated aristocrats and later for the rich bourgeois, but are now in the hands of their rightful proletarian owners. They point out the costly and useless garments and ornaments of the parasitic rich, and so forth. Religious pictures, of course, were painted for purposes of "promoting superstition."

The Isaaksky Cathedral, the greatest in Leningrad, is the third cathedral erected on this site since Catherine built the first in honour of Peter the Great. It was named Isaaksky Sobor because Peter was born on the saint's day of St. Isaac. The façade of the present building bears the inscription, "This my house is the house of prayer." Considering the present anti-religious peep-show which it now contains, this quotation might now aptly be con-

A CORDIAL BRITISH UNDERSTANDING

A Health to Mass Executions of communists, to Murders of Soviet workers, and to Destruction of Soviet institutions

tinued to the end.[1] Workers are admitted to the building at prices varying from 10 to 60 kopecks, according to their classification. Tourists pay Rs. 1.20. The chief points emphasized by our guide were as follows:

The dome of the cathedral is said to be exceeded in height only by two other cathedrals in the world—St. Peter's in Rome and SS. Peter and Paul in Leningrad. Our guide related how the present building, completed in 1858 after forty years' labour, cost 22 million roubles. A colossal bust of the architect, Montferrard, is shown; also pictures of the various artists who co-operated with him. The salary paid to each artist is printed under his picture, the amounts varying from 850,000 roubles downwards. Montferrard himself received an annual salary of 13,000 roubles, and at the end was allowed to sell the wooden scaffolding around the building; this brought him in two million roubles. The work was done mainly by "slave labour" at 50 kopecks a month. The artists' emoluments are alleged to be extravagantly disproportionate, whilst the lecturer pointed out that the whole 22 millions have been wasted, since they might have been usefully employed for workers' dwellings and for the development of industries.

The cathedral has mighty bronze doors, each weighing four tons, with numerous panels in high

[1] My house is the house of prayer: but ye have made it a den of thieves.—Luke xix. 46.

relief illustrating Biblical episodes. There are many splendid malachite and lapis-lazuli pillars, also beautiful mosaics, all by Russian artists, except two Italian examples presented by the Pope. Some of the mosaics have recently been dismounted from the ceilings and arches in which they had been erected, and transferred to easels on the floor, so that they may be better seen and enjoyed by the workers.

The main body of the cathedral is occupied by garish, tawdry stands and booths, designed for anti-religious propaganda, for which there is a specially organized department, the S.V.B. (*soyous voinstvennii bez-bozhniki*, or union of militant atheists). Amongst the numerous "side-shows" we saw the following:

Showcases containing holy relics, holy water, a sponge which dried Christ's tears, a fragment of the true Cross, etc. These were amongst the "instruments" of the Russian Church "to keep the people down." Life-sized models of priests in sacred vestments formed part of this exhibit.

Statistics were exhibited showing the "insidious growth" in the number of Russian churches from 1,400 in the year 1861 to 23,000 in 1881. These churches possessed 7,000 hectares of land, and succeeded in acquiring 30 per cent of the workers' incomes by collections, candle-fees, religious ceremonies, etc. To stimulate religious fervour, "holy men" wore iron belts and various other iron instruments of discomfort here exhibited.

The Tsarist government is accused of working hand-in-glove with the Church. We saw a large wooden ikon of St. Nicolas the "Miracle-Worker," apparently a portrait of the Tsar, whilst a photo of some particular Madonna or other was claimed to resemble the late Tsarina.

In 1905, at the time of an attempted revolution, workers were shot down by Cossacks. The names of these anti-revolutionary Cossacks are inscribed on two large silver panels exhibited to us. No panel records the names of the revolutionaries. Pictures and photos of Church processions, guarded by police clearing a way through the crowds, are also shown as examples of tyranny by the Church and Tsarist government. Another picture shows a priest blessing Russian soldiers before they departed for the front "to kill workers at the bidding of the ruling class."

In the February revolution of 1917, when the workers rose and the government fell into the hands of the bourgeoisie under Kerensky, the Church organized a procession at the funeral of the Cossacks who were killed, thereby showing its "antagonism to the workers."

Later still, during the great famine of 1921, after the Revolution, the Church was "asked" by the Bolshevik government to give up its treasures for the relief of the starving workers and peasants. The Church did not consider it advisable to do so. Accordingly the workers' government forcibly expropriated the treasures to the following amounts: 25 poods[1] of gold; 21,000 poods of silver; 82 poods of other precious metals; 33,456 diamonds, etc.

A crude illuminated transparency representing a crumbling church is shown to illustrate its present state of decay. Nowadays in Russia churches, unless supported by voluntary contributions, are either taken over for museums, schools, or commercial dining-rooms, or they are demolished for building materials for the workers.

Exhibits of various other non-official religious sects are also shown. The Eunuchs are a sect which since the middle of the nineteenth century have practised castration of males and amputation of the breasts in women. A life-sized evil-faced eunuch in a white robe is the centre of this exhibit, whilst a case of knives and razors is shown with which these sacrificial operations were performed. Also several lurid photographs of mutilated men and women.

The Feodorofists were another mystic and secret religious sect, which arose after the Revolution. Their robes, with "secret diagrams" of triangles and crosses woven in their fabric, are shown. These were considered to be anti-bolshevik because their inscription of XB (Ch-V), which to ordinary people means "Christos Voskress" (Christ is risen), can also be interpreted as Chotitye Voini (Wish for war).

[1] 1 pood = 36 lb. weight.

The Baptists, another ostensibly innocent sect, are regarded as dangerous anti-communists, who must be exterminated. Photographs of Baptists, performing baptisms in a river, holding a service in a wood, and even venturing to hold a musical party with various musical instruments, are shown as evidence against them. They "kept people away" from communism.

A picture of Churikov is also shown. This man founded a sect which was involved in subversive propaganda, e.g. to avoid alcohol, to live in a communal fashion, and to work hard. They sold holy water, however, and turned out goods too cheaply, thereby "fooling the government." Accordingly in 1928 Churikov was arrested and sent into exile, whilst his community was taken over by the government as a communal farm.

A collection of photographs of Fascists, i.e. ex-socialists who have become anti-communists, is also on exhibit. It includes Pilsudski of Poland, the Pope of Rome, and Ramsay MacDonald of England. This latter, because his hands happen to be clasped together, is pointed out as indulging in the degrading anti-communistic action of prayer. These Fascists have the additional demerit of being blessed by the Christian Church.

In a large glass case lies the black mummified body of Theodore Chernigovsky. Being discovered uncorrupted many years after his burial, he was promoted to be a saint, and 30,000 roubles were collected by the Church from devout pilgrims who came to see him. The real explanation was that the body had been buried in dry sand within a silver casket.

Various models and diagrams illustrating the truths of science and communism and the supposed fallacies of religion are also shown. Thus the Bible is alleged to teach that the earth is flat. Bruno, who taught that it was spherical, was burned at the stake, and we here see a working model of his execution with luminous red-paper flames flickering around him.

An ingenious and more convincing model, the well-known Lasalle's pendulum, to demonstrate the revolution of the earth, consists in a weight with pointer, suspended from a long string, 102 metres long, forming a huge slowly-swinging pendulum. The pointer crosses the centre of a huge disc, 20 or 30 feet broad, marked out in numerous closely set radii. Each swing of the pendulum crosses the centre of the disc in its journey from end to end of the diameter. At every swing the pendulum reaches a point on the periphery a few centimetres farther on than the previous swing. It is difficult, however, to see in what way this supports communism, or is in any way contrary to religious beliefs.

Another model shows a hollow cylindrical frame surrounded by coloured spirals, indicating the industrial decline in Germany and the U.S.A. during the last three or four years of capitalistic slump, as contrasted with the rising prosperity in communistic Russia. The German and American curves are represented as either horizontal or descending, whilst the Bolshevist spiral rises in an increasingly steep curve, without a single setback. The connection of this with religion is again difficult to follow.

Photographs of young men and women addressing audiences of workers on anti-religious subjects, are uninteresting. There is also a childish drawing of a factory worker taking excess of alcohol and then destroying his factory machinery, contrasted with another sketch illustrating the abstemiousness and efficiency of the present-day communist worker. The religious implication, if any, is again somewhat far-fetched.

At 10.30 p.m. we entrained for Moscow, a night journey of twelve hours. Twenty out of twenty-three in our party travelled "hard." Three of us were less Spartan, having paid extra to travel "soft." The "hard" passengers are herded in compartments holding sixteen, divided up by wooden shelves projecting on two levels. On these shelves grubby mattresses are spread at night. The "soft" compartments, each with four passengers, have padded couches, somewhat like the ordinary *wagon-lits*, but not quite so smart. Good mattresses and clean linen are supplied. It was well worth while paying extra, for every hard place in the train is occupied by workers in various degrees of dirt and emanation. The fourth member of our "soft" compartment was a very nice fellow, Dr. Hugo Feigl, an art expert from Prague. During the War he had been an infantry officer in the Austrian Army, which, thirty thousand in all, was captured by the Russian general, Korniloff, early in 1915. He and three hundred other Austrian officers were interned in a prison-camp in Turkistan for three years. He himself then developed "barbed-wire" psychosis, and felt he could not stand it any longer. He succeeded in escaping across the Polish frontier, after a six thousand miles journey across the south of Russia and the Caspian Sea, disguised sometimes as a bolshevik, sometimes as a merchant. He now buys art treasures in Russia on behalf of big galleries in Berlin, Prague, and America.

The countryside from Leningrad to Moscow is a fertile plain, dotted with farms, villages, and growing towns. Even at 6 a.m. crowds of intending passengers thronged all the stations. We passed a military aerodrome with deep, narrow, quadrilateral trenches for refuge against air attacks. Many farmers' houses are wooden huts, like our military huts, perched on trestles to keep them cool in summer and out of the snow in winter.

CHAPTER III

MOSCOW

Moscow is a busier and more thronged city than Leningrad. The people are not different in appearance from ordinary Europeans. They are healthy looking, clean, comfortably dressed, and mostly young. A few horses and an occasional camel are seen in the streets. Otherwise all the traffic consists of noisy electric trams, buses, and a few tourist cars owned by the Touring Agency.

We spent part of our first afternoon listening to a long Russian lecture in an Institute of Health and Social Hygiene. The director, a Hebrew gentleman, expounded at great and wearisome length the activities and objects of his Institute. This was organised in 1922 under the department of health for the study of subjects such as planning of hospitals and dispensaries, the health conditions of factories and schools, the publication of statistics (Russians wallow in statistics and percentages) relating to tuberculosis, occupational diseases, etc. It also teaches its students how to compose suitable slogans and posters for combined health and communistic propaganda. It has a two years' post-graduate course for qualified medical men who will subsequently become professors and teachers in various universities and institutes. These workers were all on vacation. Prior to the War, this building had been a private abortorium. We were shown nothing of the actual working, and everything could have been told us in ten minutes. Altogether most of this time was wasted, except perhaps for our lady guide, who understood and enjoyed the whole lecture, of which she communicated short snatches in English to us at long intervals.

A hasty scramble through the town followed this dreary show. We careered at full speed past the ancient Chinese wall with its pointed loopholes and crenellated parapet, built by the ancient Muscovite merchants to protect the mercantile quarter against wandering tribes, the nobles being safely housed within the Kremlin. Several ancient churches are now in process of being demolished, including the great Church of the Redeemer which is to be replaced by a Soviet Palace. Another church is labelled with a red banner as "*stolovaya*," or public dining-room. We had a passing glimpse of the bronze statue of the great surgeon Pirogoff, erected outside a row of clinics established by him in the old days; also of an ornate nunnery, the *novo-dyevichi*, with high red-brick wall and golden-domed church within, now a feminist museum. There are endless blocks of workers flats; some of these are entirely new, others have been constructed by adding three or four stories of plain stone-work on the top of three or four stories of ornate pre-revolutionary architecture. One big building is a communistic academy for the training of Red professors. Kropotkin Street, a street of aristocratic palaces, is now transformed into museums, institutes, galleries, and a club for scientists. We were shown the headquarters of the Communist International, also the First Moscow University, near a great square with the Red statue of Liberty, around whose base are huge bronze panels—a sort of ten tables of the commandments, recording the original declaration and pronouncements of the communistic constitution. These panels are cast from bronze obtained by the melting down of a statue of Alexander II which formerly stood here. In Pushkin Square is a statue of the poet; at another side is the beautiful Moscow theatre and an anti-religious museum. The Arch of Triumph, surmounted by a quadriga, commemorating the victory of Alexander II over Napoleon, has not yet been marked for destruction. Alexander Square, now called the White Russia Square, is where the railway station stands, belonging to railways leading to France and Germany. A racecourse, aerodrome, and sports stadium replace what was formerly the Imperial park. A statue has been erected to Vorovski, a Soviet ambassador who was assassinated in Switzerland a few years ago. On and on, through streets with fine shop windows, now only selling fruit, toys, beer, and junk.

Last of all, we came to the huge Red Square. This is flanked on one side by the crenellated towered wall of the Kremlin, and along the south side by the remarkable Cathedral of St. Basil, with nine churches under a single roof, to commemorate Alexander's nine great victories. Near the centre of the square is a large circular white marble platform, *Labnoye myesto*, or Place of the Skull, formerly the place of public executions.

Then there is a great squat, massive rectangular building of superimposed strata of deep-red stone. This is LENIN'S TOMB. Its bronze doors are guarded by bayoneted Red guards. Above the entrance is the name ЛЕНИН in huge capitals on a black marble lintel. Thousands of people, men, women, and children, are queued up along the square, waiting to get in. The daily attendance is said to be about ten thousand persons. We joined the throng and were admitted at once, this being a courtesy extended to parties of foreigners when expected in advance. We enter a dark broad corridor, and walk in single file down granite steps. Every few yards stands an armed Red guard, who scrutinizes each visitor closely in passing. Then at the bottom we turn to the left and reach the central tomb of the mausoleum. Here lies Lenin himself, embalmed, under a great glass canopy of prismatic shape, brightly illuminated. He is very like himself as shown in popular pictures and statues—bald head, stubbly moustache, reddish pointed beard, forceful chin, widely separated eyes, and short pug nose. He is dressed in a badly fitting khaki tunic with a red rosette pinned on the left breast. The hands lie in the lap, clutching rather pathetically at emptiness. The lower part of the trunk is not seen, being covered with a dull-coloured sort of cloth, over which a long crape scarf is coiled in serpentine folds.

I looked carefully at the head, especially behind the ears, to see if there were any signs of the usual autopsy incisions for removal of the brain (which has already been cut in serial sections by Vogt, the German neuro-pathologist). But I saw no marks of incisions; these may have been skilfully concealed. Or perhaps it may be, as some people hint, that this is really an elaborate wax model? The original body, it may be remembered, was withdrawn from exhibition some time ago for about eighteen months, for purposes of re-embalming and preservation. Be this as it may, the sight is most impressive, not only the body of the dead Lenin, but the thousands of silent Lenin worshippers filing past the catafalque, day after day, year after year.

Lenin Worship

The apotheosis and cult of Lenin in Soviet Russia amounts to a new religion. Statues and pictures of Lenin, large and small, decorate every factory, museum, restaurant, and hospital; also most shop windows and nearly every worker's home. Slogans extracted from his speeches, emblazoned in white letters on red banners, are displayed not only on the walls but also on tramways and buses and in hospital wards. Even in an infants' hospital, which contained no child over three years of age, we saw a communistic slogan on the wall. Quotations of Lenin's words, the new Leninist gospel, are analogous to the scriptural texts which adorn devout homes in England. Every factory and every ship has its "Lenin Corner," a sort of communist chapel with a bust of Lenin and pictures of his satellite saints, Stalin, Djerjinsky, Liebknecht, etc., together with a wall-newspaper containing fiery communistic news and propaganda.

The Holy of Holies is the Lenin Tomb in the Red Square at Moscow, where thousands of Lenin worshippers daily file past his embalmed body. In far country districts, wild bards chant hymns of praise, singing of tractors and revolutions, of land reform, and, most of all, of Lenin himself, calling upon him to come back from the dead and lead them once more to victory. The annexed examples of these new folk songs (quoted from V.O.K.S. No. 1, 1932) show the rising tide of Lenin idolatry.

1. A KIRGHIZ SONG

In Moscow, the great stone-built city
Where all the people's chiefs are gathered,
In the heart of the city is a tent,
And therein reposes Lenin.

If thou be sad and weary
And nothing console thee,
Come hither to this tent
And gaze on Lenin.

And thy sadness will thaw like water,
And thy grief will float away like leaves borne by the stream;
And a new—quiet—sadness will possess thee
As thou gazest on him who was the country's father
And was hurt by the sting of death.

From our steppes
We raise a sorrowful groan,
For dead is Lenin,
And never will there be another one like him.

We love Lenin as we love our steppes.
Nay, even more—we would give away
All our tents and steppes,
All our camels and wives and children,
Only to bring him back,
But his awesome whereabouts is dark and unknown . . .

Where shall we seek him?
And we cry, and the steppe cries with us . . .
And the moon and the stars weep with us . . .
They remember Lenin. We remember Lenin.
And never shall we nor our grand-children's grand-children
Forget him. . . . Thick grass will grow upon our steppes,
And scores of Kirghiz generations will pass over the earth,
Yet the last of them—when dying—will feel happy
In going thither—to meet Lenin.

(*English translation by* M. L. KORR.)

2. A TADJIK FOLK SONG

"What Hafizes Sing About"

We, Tadjiks, sing of that which we see and which sets our mind on singing. . . .
If we see a pretty horse we sing a song about it;
This song will be known only by those who sing it, and the rest will never know about this song.
This will happen because horses worthy of songs are many, very many, and everyone will sing about the one he has seen himself.

But we have songs that are composed by sweet-voiced Hafizes
And these songs are intended to travel across the boundaries of years, and sometimes centuries.

Such songs, surviving three centuries, were sung by Firkat, and later, by Nahani:
They sang about beautiful women and flowers.

Now we have many Hafizes, little inferior to Firkat and Nahani,
But these Hafizes sing not about beautiful women and flowers;
They sing about the new freedom,
They sing about the airplane.
They sing about the blissful life of the future,
But most of all they sing about Lenin.
And this they do because without Lenin no songs would have been born
Save such as resemble the yelling of dogs, that is, such as praised the Tsar Nikolai,
And his generals, colonels, and soldiers.
Lenin gave the Hafizes the right to sing about anything they liked,
And forthwith they began to sing about him.

(*English translation by* M. L. Korr.)

3. A FERGHANA FOLK SONG

Many we are on this earth set free by Lenin:
Uzbeks, Urus, Tadjiks, and other peoples.
All of us have in our blood a drop of Lenin's blood.
And we will defend our freedom.

Our swords are keen and bright,
Our rifles are loaded,
Our guns are ready for the fray.
We have saddled our war-horses.

And in the battle soon a-coming,
Mightly Lenin will come down to us from on high,
And his fiery sword will shine with a new light,
And the whole world will hear his thundering words.

He will march in front of us,
And we will rush behind him upon our enemies,
Like a storm that spares nought and nought can stop it.
Much blood will there be, and our foes will be beaten,
And they will flee before our forces.

But we, with Lenin, will march ever onward,
And with Lenin's name we will rouse all the slaves;
To the old there will be no return,
And a new sun will rise over the earth.

(*English translation by* M. L. KORR.)

To the list of great prophets such as Buddha, Moses, Paul, and Mahomet must now be added the name of Lenin.

In the Moscow *Daily News* to-day we read that England and the various Dominions at the Ottawa conference have just reached an agreement to restrict foreign trade "in a vain attempt to hold the British Empire together." The British Press is said to be "dismayed."

I called at the British Embassy, where in the absence of the ambassador, Sir Esmond Ovey, I was very kindly received by his chief attaché, Mr. Strang. He invited myself and F. G. to lunch next day, and gave us many useful hints as to how to make the most of our time in Moscow.

The hotel food and service have deteriorated since Leningrad. It took us three-quarters of an hour after sitting down to lunch before the first course was served, and another three-quarters for the rest of the three-course meal to arrive. The bedrooms, however, are clean, and all of them are fitted with bathrooms, some of which, on the lower floors, have running water.

August 23rd

We visited a MARRIAGE AND DIVORCE OFFICE. An outer waiting-room is placarded with coloured diagrams and propagandist posters concerning sex hygiene and the necessity for pre-marital medical examination, also explaining about venereal diseases and the various modes of non-genital infection. Some of these are strongly anti-religious, e.g. pictures of the risks of infection by the sacramental cup, by circumcision, by sprinkling with holy water, by the *Christos Voskress*" Easter kiss, also the danger of infant baptism by immersion. There are also posters describing the diseases hindering normal sex life, and the chief diseases contra-indicating marriage: syphilis, gonorrhoea, and tuberculosis. Finally, there are diagrams of child-welfare—sunshine, suitable clothing, etc., together with lurid pictures showing the effects of alcoholic excess and of tuberculosis upon married life.

Marriage registration and divorce are performed in an inner room, hung with pictures of Lenin and Marx. The registration is executed by a girl clerk, who questions the parties and fills up the necessary identification papers, including the name, age, nationality, occupation, and present address of each prospective spouse. Both parties must sign a declaration that the registration is a voluntary affair, that they are cognisant of the laws of marriage and divorce, and that they have been informed of the state of each other's health. A certificate is then issued to both parties. The fee for each union-worker is two roubles; to those who are not members of a trade-union it is ten roubles.

Divorce registration is carried out at the same table. It is not necessary for both parties to be present. A record is made of the number of children, if any, of the marriage, and as to whether the child is self-supporting, and, if not, which of the parents will be responsible for its care. A charge of two or ten roubles is made, according to the same scale as the registration department.

A well-equipped abortorium was then visited. This consists of a suite of rooms on the first floor. A central ante-room is hung with dramatic pictures of the female genital organs, also large coloured diagrams of curettage. There are bottles containing human foetuses at various stages up to three months. There is also a picture of a badly performed abortion, causing perforation of the uterus, followed by infection, intense suffering, finally showing a coffin drawn on a sleigh, whilst another picture shows a skilful and successful abortion, with the woman back at her work in a few days.

Above the doorway leading into the preliminary shaving department hangs a placard, "The abortion performed here to-day should be the last." Another says, "Those who do not wish for a child should practise contraception." Coloured models illustrating well-fitting and ill-fitting cervical caps are shown. On the wall opposite to the first placard hangs a charming engraving of a beautiful young mother and child, marked "Mon Tresor."

The director, Dr. Madjulick, explained in excellent German that he has a staff of six doctors, each of whom carries out ten successive abortion operations, i.e. a daily total of sixty. The duration of each operation averages seven minutes. The ages of the abortees vary from twenty to thirty-five years. Before admission to the abortorium, each patient is examined at a gynaecological clinic, where the risks of abortion are explained to her, any medical contra-indications are inquired for, also the social reasons for the abortion. No inquiry is made as to whether the woman is married or not, this being a matter of entire unconcern. Poorer women are treated free; others pay from 8 up to 40 roubles, according to the salary and social expenses of the worker. Abortions are performed from the fifth up to the twelfth week of pregnancy, after which stage of pregnancy the affair must go on to term without intervention. Each patient stays in hospital until the third day, when she is discharged.

In the five years since 1926 the number of abortions in this clinic has risen from 2,000 to 11,000. No deaths occurred last year. The number of septic infections is very small. There were two cases of pelvic peritonitis and two of perforated uteri with immediate suture.

Fifty per cent of the abortion patients are brain-workers, about 8 per cent being students. Of the remaining 50 per cent the great majority are factory workers. Only about 10 per cent of the total belong to the peasant class. Abortion, therefore, is mainly a city luxury.

The abortion-rate for all Russia in 1931 was stated to us by the vice-chairman of V.O.K.S. as 8·2 per 1,000 population. This confirms the foregoing figures and means that it is much higher in the urban than in the industrial population. The birth-rate varies from 29·5 in the city of Moscow to 38·8 in country districts.

We witnessed a couple of these curettages. The patient walks in and climbs on to the operating-table. The doctor does the antiseptic washing and douching with lysoform lotion. The uterus is then rapidly dilated by graduated dilators and thoroughly curetted. No intra-uterine irrigation is carried out. No anaesthetic is used. The first patient whom we saw was a woman of twenty-four, a cook, seven weeks pregnant, who was having her second abortion, in spite of the warning placard. She appeared to suffer only moderate discomfort from the dilators, which caused her to grimace at times but not to call out.

A LAW-COURT is an unpretentious room. We saw a court in which an appeal was being made against a conviction by a lower court. A co-operative-store worker had been charged and convicted of having stolen vodka from the store, consuming large quantities himself and selling the remainder to his fellow-workers at a high price. The judge was a youngish middle-aged woman sitting on a dais, supported by two white-coated young men—"apprentice judges." One of these read the record of the previous proceedings in the lower court and the alleged grounds of appeal. The appellant stood up and was examined and cross-examined by the judge for a few minutes. A question was also asked by one of the assistants. The judge confirmed the findings of the lower court, and when we left was busy inquiring into the appellant's financial and social standing. Our guide informs us that such a culprit will be punished, not by imprisonment, but by a fine to be deducted from his wages for a term of weeks. He will also be transferred to work in future in a different co-operative store.

The judge in this court is said to be professionally trained. The assistant, or apprentice judges, are students at a training college, acquiring practical experience.

A prophylactorium against prostitution is one of a group of institutions organized since 1925 to try and get rid of the 25,000 prostitutes who then lived in Moscow. The factory workers organized delegations of women workers to canvas these women in the streets, and persuade them to enter a prophylactorium. There is no compulsion to enter the institution, unless patients have some venereal disease, in which case they must go to a special clinic. In these homes the prostitutes are taught useful occupations—sewing, knitting, and workshop activities. After a stay of six to ten months the inmates are placed in vacant posts at different factories, where the committee still keeps in touch with them. Relapses to the streets are uncommon. Obstinate and relapsing cases are "sent away to remote places."

Workers' Dwellings

An apartment was visited in one of the newest blocks. This apartment had three small living-rooms with a good bathroom and a nice little kitchen; it was inhabited by three adults and four children. A private W.C. was utilized also for purposes of storing odds and ends. Beds were in every living-room, and also in the kitchen. Everything was neat and tidy, and the furniture comfortable. The grandmother, who lives at home, does nearly all the housework, whilst the mother does a special clean-up on her sixth day off-work as a cashier. The husband is a student. For the foregoing apartment the ordinary rent is 60 roubles a month; but the man was a "Red hero" during the revolution, and therefore gets it at 50 per cent reduction. Electric light is extra. The telephone costs 10 roubles a month. For each block of flats there is a local committee or soviet which deals with any complaints from individual tenants. A skilled sanitary inspector can be called in to advise, if necessary.

We then went, on our own initiative, a hundred yards across a piece of waste ground, to see workers' apartments in a large converted pre-revolutionary house, formerly occupied by the director of a factory. The picture was quite different. A central entrance lobby is only lighted in the daytime when the door is open. Off this opens a communal kitchen with an ancient tiled stove; five oil-stoves, one for each tenant on that floor, are set out on a ledge. The floor is dirty. The living-rooms, arranged in five pairs, one for each set of tenants, are divisions partitioned off what had once been three large rooms. Some of them open into a communal dark corridor; others are reached by penetrating from one to another *en suite*. There is no bathroom. One pitch-dark and noisome cellar hidden under the staircase forms a communal sanitary cubicle for the five families. Electric light is laid on, but there is no water in the building; it has to be fetched by hand from a well a few hundred yards away. For these apartments each set of tenants pays 7 to 15 roubles a month, depending on their income. Of course, this being a converted building, one could not expect the same conveniences as in a modern block of apartments, but the overcrowding was bad, and any epidemic disease would spread like wildfire.

We had a delightful lunch at the British Embassy at the invitation of Mr. Strang, the senior attaché. The Embassy is in a magnificent house standing in its own gardens, formerly occupied by a rich merchant. In addition to ourselves, the other guests were Mr. R.-S., a member of Lord M's party whom we had met before on the boat, and Mr. A. C., an agricultural expert from Winnipeg, who has been travelling up and down Russia for several months, studying the farming conditions, this being his second visit. He tells me that the government statistics on the subject of production of food products are exaggerations to the extent of at least 30 per cent. The agricultural department is run by young communists at headquarters without any knowledge of practical farming. The individual farming groups are managed by young men of twenty-two to twenty-four years of age, also without previous experience. The best workers are the despised "kulaks," who have been forced by the pressure of hunger to join these collective farms, having previously been evicted from their own private farms.

There are three main classes of farms. First, the State farms, or "*Sovchoz*," staffed and over-staffed with "workers" at a monthly wage. These farms are a dead loss, in spite of the mechanical tractors and other equipment supplied by the government. Second, the collective farms, or "*Kolchoz*," cultivated by peasants and ex-kulaks who work together.

There are three subdivisions of these collective farms: (*a*) *Tovaristchwo* or Comrade farms (11 per cent), in which individual peasants, owning cattle or machinery (the State now owns all the land), lend their stock or equipment to the community, and share in the community profits, according to work done by each. (*b*) *Artel* or partnership farms (80 per cent), in which adjacent peasants pool their live-stock and equipment, individual families being allowed to keep a cow or so, also chickens. The community buys the live-stock or machinery from the peasant. If he has nothing to contribute to the common stock, he may enter as a shareholder at a fee of 5 to 25 roubles. Some poorer peasants are admitted free, if during their previous career they have not been traders or "exploiters." (*c*) Communal type of collective farms (7 per cent) in which everything in the form of live-stock, tools, etc., is common property. The workers live in communal dwellings, with communal kitchens, dining-rooms, crêches, etc.

The standard of farming in these collective farms, except in the German-speaking district of the Volga, where Germans have lived for four hundred years, is deplorable. Owing to want of proper ploughing, the crops are heavily overgrown with weeds, so that when the combined tractor, reaper, and thresher comes along, the wheat is mixed with rubbish and extra labour is required to winnow it out. Also the grain is moist from overhanging weeds, and consequently the resulting flour is inferior in quality. It will take years of farming to clean up the ground again and make it fit for good production.

Lastly, there are a few small private farms managed by individual peasants, formerly prohibited, but which within the last few months the government has again permitted to be run, on condition that a stipulated quota of grain is forthcoming, just as from the collective farms. This quota is claimed before the farmers get any grain for themselves. For the grain the government pays a fixed price, of 1 to 6 roubles per pood, most often only 1 rouble. The excess, if any, which the peasants are allowed to sell, has a value in the open market of at least 90 and sometimes 150 roubles per pood, i.e. the government pays one-ninetieth of the market price to the producer. The collectivized peasant, whose horses have been either pooled or slaughtered, and who has not yet learned to be expert in the management of a tractor, struggles along under increasingly bad conditions of the land which he tries to cultivate. The ill-fed peasants are becoming more and more restless and resentful, feeling that they are being robbed by the government.

The MUSEUM OF THE REVOLUTION is housed in a large building which was formerly the English Club in Moscow. This historical museum is for the purpose of illustrating the growth and progress of class war, of socialism, and finally of communism in Russia. Being designed for popular propaganda, largely of an emotional type, it is necessarily crude in many respects, but specially suitable on this account for mass tuition. The main story, as related to us, runs as follows:

The workers began to be openly restless about the seventeenth century, when their first great uprising took place under the leadership of Stepan Razin, a Don cossack from the Volga. The insurrection of serfs under his leadership for a time had some success. Ultimately, however, he was defeated, captured, and brought to Moscow, where he was publicly executed, his hands, feet, and head being chopped off in succession. Bright pictures of these executions are shown.

In the eighteenth century, about 1774, Pugachoff led another uprising of serfs. This was successfully repressed by Catherine the Great, the portrait of whom, a benevolent-looking lady, is hung beside a contemporary engraving of Pugachoff confined in an iron cage. In this he was brought to Moscow, where his cage was chained to the Kremlin wall as a warning to the populace. He was duly hanged. Knouts, branding-irons marking K.A.T., are exhibited, also collections of chains and fetters. There is a large picture of Pugachoff in the days of his success, condemning a richly clad landowner brought before him by the serfs. Pugachoff issued a manifesto permitting the serfs to shave their beards, to pay lower taxes, to possess land, to have fishing rights, etc. There is an old oil-painting of Pugachoff found in a landowner's house, picturing Pugachoff consumed with remorse for his uprising, with the fires of hell briskly burning in the background.

The dominion of landowners over their serfs at this time was absolute (just as in America), with legal rights of buying and selling them like cattle. A contemporary placard is shown, setting forth the domestic accomplishments of a young woman offered for sale as a special bargain. There is also a striking oil-painting of a beautiful young actress, from whom her baby has been taken away to another corner of the barn, whilst she is being forced to suckle a puppy.

Early in the nineteenth century the Decabrist risings began. These were led by bourgeois and educated men. This outbreak failed. Many leaders were executed in 1826, and others were sent to Siberia. Meanwhile the living conditions of the serfs continued to deteriorate, and repeated uprisings continued until 1861, when Alexander II proclaimed liberation of the serfs, with freedom to own their land and to move from their place of birth if they so desired. He announced to the antagonistic landowners that it was wiser that freedom should come from above rather than await revolution from below. The material improvement of the peasant's lot, however, was not yet satisfactory. Repeated uprisings continued, and in 1872 the First International Meeting of Reformers was held, under the chairmanship of Karl Marx. The intelligentsia of Russia now became politically minded, and began agitating for democracy. Even some aristocrats like Prince Kropotkin joined the reforming party, also numerous students and professional men.

During the nineteenth century the power of capitalism rapidly increased, contrary to the predictions of Karl Marx. A new class of underpaid factory workers arose. The intelligentsia leaders of the revolutionary movement organized an agitation not only amongst the peasants but also by the industrial workers. Such propaganda were "underground," closely pursued and rigidly repressed by the Russian police. Many revolutionary leaders were betrayed by the peasants. There is a picture of Sophia Perovskaya, who was executed after making one of the many attempts to assassinate Alexander II. (The twelfth attempt was successful.) Also one of Vera Figner. The revolutionaries at this time were divided into two groups: the terrorist group, who used bombs, etc., and the "black soil" group, who preferred peaceful agitation and propaganda.

Now began the Social Democratic movement, contemporary with the growing power of capitalism. Plechanoff, a follower of Marx, proclaimed in 1889 that a revolution of the workers was the only practical possibility for securing a remedy of their grievances. Under capitalism the workers' wages did not rise proportionately to the profits earned by them for the employers. A large painting is shown of a bloated capitalist paying a trifling wage to an indignant employee. The first industrial strike in Russia was at the Morozoff factory in 1885.

About 1893 the revolutionists organized numerous small "circles," under the guidance of Lenin, then a young advocate, and his fellow-worker Samara, with the idea of developing from these circles a wider spread mass agitation. We see a photograph of a group showing Lenin and his fellow-workers (in 1895), mostly students, together with several engineers—all educated men. A model is also shown of the wooden house in Minsk where the First Congress of the Russian Social Democratic Party was held. Its leaders were promptly arrested, imprisoned, and exiled. Underground propaganda, however, continued, largely by means of leaflets printed on secret presses. Specimens are shown of revolutionary articles by the Jewish Bund stereotyped in paper pulp for exportation to Russia. These leaflets were ingeniously smuggled in various ways, e.g. by placing them at the backs of mirrors, etc. (Specimens shown.)

The revolutionary agitation continued. Political slogans were devised. The first of these, carried on a banner in 1903 at a public demonstration, was "Long Live the International Russian Social Democratic Party." Others were "Down with Monarchy. Long Live Freedom. Long Live the Eight-Hour Day. Long Live Social Democracy."

Increasing numbers of strikes (shown by curves and diagrams) were now led by the workers themselves and not by the intelligentsia. Pictures are shown of dispersals of such strikes and processions by troops, also a photograph of a group of wounded processionists in hospital. There is a contemporary engraving of the "pyramid of society," resting on the shoulders of the workers at the foot. On top is a monarch, whose motto is "We are Reigning Over You." Next the government officials, "We are Ruling You." Then the priests, "We are Deceiving You." Then the soldiers, "We are Shooting You." Then the bourgeoisie, "We are Eating You." And lowest of all, the worker, "We are Working for You; We are Feeding You." A slogan of this period runs as follows: "There will come a time when the people will awaken. We shall heave our shoulders and, with the united force of our comrades, overthrow the whole edifice."

During this time of increasing uprisings of workers and peasants Lenin was in exile. A photograph is shown of the suburban villa in London where Lenin lived during 1902–3. Here he edited a revolutionary journal, *Iskra*, the *Spark*, which was stereotyped in England and the stereos sent out to Russia for underground propaganda. The *Iskra* exercised a powerful influence on the Russian workers, some of whom in 1901 sent back the following message, "Everything is ready. Only a spark is needed to kindle the flames. Teach us fighting and the technique of fighting."

In 1903 the second congress of Brussels–Paris took place. Here the revolutionists split into two divisions, Menshevists and Bolshevists, with differences in their respective programmes. Trotsky was one of the Menshevists. Lenin and Plechnakoff were among the Bolshevists, who were a majority. The

Bolshevists announced that a good worker must not only pay a subscription towards the party; he must take an active part. Unanimity of the party and expulsion of all dissentient members were enforced.

During the Russo–Japanese War of 1905 the workers were still further oppressed by the capitalists.

In January 1903, on "bloody Sunday," a petition and procession to the Tsar, led by a priest, Gapon, was organized in Petersburg at the Winter Palace. The Tsar did not appear, and the unarmed processionists were shot down by troops. Lenin now announced, "The workers have now had the lesson of civil war. Revolutionary education has made a greater step in advance than would have been possible in months or years." The people despaired of peaceful revolution, and lost faith in the good will of the Tsar.

In 1903 the Third International bolshevik party started to organize the proletariat for an armed uprising. Propaganda were carried out in the Army and Navy. In 1905 occurred the mutiny on board the cruiser *Potemkin.* The crew overpowered the officers and, under the command of a sailor, Matuchenko, sailed back and forth in the Black Sea until recaptured by the government forces. Photographs are shown of this cruise, of the officers, and of the mutineers.

The strikes in factories, railways, etc., continued

to increase in number, until in one year, 1903, there were 1,700,000 strikers. Secret codes and ciphers of the revolutionaries are shown.

Then came the "first manifesto" by Nicholas II, granting freedom of speech, etc. Trepoff, however, the Minister of Justice, promptly issued another manifesto threatening to use arms and ammunition unhesitatingly against the revolutionaries. A copy of this manifesto is shown with a large scarlet hand-print across it—"the bloody hand of Trepoff." (This was a revolutionary embellishment to the poster.)

Workers and strikers attacked factories, whilst peasants attacked the landowners' houses, as shown in photographs and pictures. There is a large statue of a worker picking up a huge stone with which to fight. Street fighting occurred in Moscow. Pictures are shown of Cossacks attacking the fleeing mob with knouts. Fighting went on behind barricades in the Krasnoi Presni, a textile quarter of Moscow, under the leadership of Poliakoff.

The revolt of 1903 having been suppressed by Tsarist troops, Plechnoff now urged that strikers must arm themselves, the workers in this revolt having learned the lessons of civil war destined to encourage them in the successful revolt of 1923.

There is a large picture emblematic of these uprisings, showing the Imperial crown shaken in 1905 and again in 1907, but not yet overthrown, whilst at the other end of the picture is a serrated cockscomb-like outline, disappearing into the horizon and indicating the triumph of communism.

Next came the Great War of 1914–18. Pictures are shown of contemporary communist leaders, including Liebknecht and Rosa Luxembourg.

In 1917 a combined force of soldiers, sailors, and workers captured the Winter Palace in Petrograd, and Kerensky, of whom a caricature is shown, became temporary ruler of the new Provisional Government. Meanwhile Lenin had arrived in Petrograd in a closed railway carriage from Switzerland, making a long detour *via* Sweden and Finland. He arrived in April 1917, and at once resumed energetic personal propaganda amongst the workers, demanding the immediate cessation of the war with Germany and proclaiming the future brotherhood of peoples. No mention is made of his colleague, Trotsky, who was equally prominent at this time. Fresh Bolshevist demonstrations in the streets during June 1917 were shot down by Kerensky troops. The workers became exasperated, and at last the Winter Palace, occupied at that time by the Kerensky government, was shelled by Bolshevist troops from the Peter and Paul fortress, and by the guns of a naval cruiser in the Neva, whose crew had joined the movement. The Kerensky government was captured, and its members were imprisoned in the political casemates of Peter and Paul. Kerensky himself escaped to England.

The Soviet government, now in power, concluded

an ignominious peace with the Kaiser by the treaty of Brest-Litovsk. Civil war between the Soviet army and the various White Russian forces under Denikin, Wrangel, Koltchak, etc., continued for a time. Various expeditionary forces, from France, England, Italy, Czecho-slovakia, and the U.S.A. intervened in Russian territories in 1920. Eventually all of these, failing to achieve the defeat of the Soviet government forces in Russia, withdrew. The Red Army of workers and peasants, organized in 1928, has since held the field. Stands of flags captured from various interventionist forces are shown. It is specially pointed out that these are all of different colours, whilst the Soviet flags, shown in another stand, are uniformly red. Some of the primitive field-guns employed in Siberia to fight the anti-revolutionary army are shown, including an ingenious wooden rattle which imitated the noise of a machine-gun.

In 1924 a great famine occurred throughout the Volga country. The Soviet government appealed to the Russian Church to sell its treasures for the relief of the starving peasantry. The ecclesiastical authorities refused, and accordingly all churches were forcibly despoiled.

No reference is made to the numerous well-authenticated atrocities perpetrated by the Soviet government, and especially by the notorious Tche-Ka (Extraordinary Commission) from 1917 onward, which executed in cold blood not only Tsarist soldiers and officers, bishops and priests, helpless professional men and landowners, but also thousands of unarmed men, women, and boys.[1] Nor are any pictures shown of the notorious Soviet prison camps with their overcrowded, starving inmates, particulars of which have been recorded and corroborated by the few prisoners who succeeded in escaping.[2]

After the period of civil strife comes the present period of reconstruction. This is copiously illustrated by diagrams, posters, and models, especially of the Five-Year Plan, initiated in 1927, whereby Soviet Russia is now organizing all her own heavy industries, comprising coal, steel, machinery, electrical power, etc., so as to make her independent of capitalist countries. A dramatic curve is shown to illustrate the continuous rise in Russian industries, compared with the slower rise and subsequent slump in capitalist countries like the U.S.A., Germany, France, and England. A placard sets forth the following reasons why the Five-Year Plan cannot fail to succeed:

(1) It is a planned system.

(2) The workers are working collectively, and for themselves.

(3) Former unproductive expenses are now abolished, including the cost of the Royal Family,

[1] *The Red Terror in Russia,* by S. P. Melgounov. J. M. Dent & Sons, 1925.

[2] *An Island Hell: A Soviet Prison in the Far North,* by S. A. Malsagoff. A. M. Philpot, Ltd., 1926.

the Church, industrial loans, and bourgeois extravagance.

(4) Diminished expenditure on armaments.

Models are shown illustrating the progressive and continuous increase in production of steel, coal, textile goods, etc.[1] There is also a diagram of the numerous electric power stations and radio stations now being erected all over Russia.

There is a model of the Tsarist political prison, formerly situated at Schlüsselberg. We also see a life-size reproduction of a cell in the Peter and Paul fortress with the actual wooden door of Kamera No. 26, where Vera Figner was imprisoned. There are samples of iron shackles for the wrists and ankles, which political prisoners were compelled to wear during their journey to Siberia, walking all the way. There is also a photograph of a monument inscribed with the names of various political prisoners who died in Schlüsselberg.

As an exhibition, this is a dramatic and logically arranged historical exposition of the rise of Marxian–Leninist communism, looked at from the communistic angle, and specially designed to arouse anger and contempt for the old régime. Most of the paintings and statuary of any real artistic value have been obtained by the "nationalization" of landlords' country houses, monasteries, and

[1] These are grossly inaccurate, as regards coal at any rate, according to the statements of one of their own commisars, Kuybishev (see p. 173).

churches. These private possessions were previously "inaccessible" for museum purposes.

We visited a collective farm belonging to the Artel type (see p. 92). It has a board of seven directors, one of whom is chairman, elected by the 229 families, who have a total population of 630. Another central committee is elected to "observe and check-up" the directors. These directors and committee are elected for a year, after which they may offer themselves for re-election. This particular community farm, occupying 200 hectares of land, raises chiefly cabbages, tomatoes, and pigs. It possesses 80 horses. Two tractors, loaned or hired from a district office, do the ploughing, and have already ploughed 75 hectares. Each tractor ploughs 7 hectares in 24 hours, working 24 hours on end in three shifts. The working plan for each year is drawn up by the board of directors. In addition there are 7 "field-brigades" to stimulate and supervise the work in the 7 subdivisions of the estate. The leaders of these field-brigades are specially trained for two months before taking up their "gingering" duties.

The gross receipts for the year 1931 were stated at 667,000 roubles received from the co-operative stores, to which all produce must be sold. Of this total, 3 per cent was handed over as Government tax; 35 per cent was used partly for repayment and interest on Government loans, partly for capital improvements, such as new glass cucumber-frames.

The remainder was shared between the workers, men and women, at the rate of about 4·35 roubles per day, more or less, according to the so-called "labour-day," i.e. the quantity and quality of the day's work, as judged by the field-brigades. During the present year 1932 the privilege of selling a proportion of the produce in the open market has again been conceded. An "agronomical" expert occasionally visits the farm to give special advice.

This particular farm secured the first prize in the Moscow district for the quantity and quality of its produce. Its yield was 42 tons of cabbages per hectare and 22 tons of cucumbers per hectare.

We reached the farm along a very bad country road, full of pot-holes. The collective settlement consists of a village of wooden houses and huts. Some of the houses have characteristic elaborate Russian carvings around their window-frames and the lintels of the doors; evidently in the old days they had belonged to well-to-do farmers. They are now dilapidated, dirty, and falling to pieces, many of them with roofs partly gone, others with a wall caved in. The gardens adjoining these houses are dirty and untidy. Black mattresses and grubby sheets hang from the branches of the trees. The fields of cabbages and tomatoes are choked with weeds and thistles. The appearance of the fields would break the heart of any ordinary farmer. The whole outlook is miserable and disorderly, worse than anything I ever saw, even in war-stricken villages in the no-man's-land of Macedonia.

The children of the collective farm are educated communally. Mothers are delivered in the local hospital, not in their own homes, by a midwife, who may call in a doctor if in difficulties.

The village baby-farm is lodged in one of the former farmhouses. It contains thirty clean but puny infants, all of whom have been born in the village maternity home. Their little wicker cots are closely packed into two rooms. Farther along the village is the kindergarten, where in another converted farmhouse twenty-four children, from one-and-a-half to three years of age, are being looked after by a country girl, whose chief duty seems to be to sing proletarian songs and try to get the little ones to join in the choruses. They sat around two large tables about two feet high, looking wistful and cowed, evidently eagerly awaiting their midday meal. These children sleep on stretchers, perched on low trestles, touching each other at the sides. The whole village is a picture of dirt and decay.

A visit to the "House for the Peasant" in Moscow was somewhat wearisome. This is a museum and institution for instructing in agricultural methods any peasants who may be passing through Moscow. Similar institutions exist in other towns, but on a less elaborate scale. The museum has a residential club attached. The building, before the revolution, had been a restaurant. There are diagrams and models of agricultural methods and farm buildings, also of veterinary maladies and human diseases specially liable to occur among peasants. There are elementary anatomical posters and diagrams, with special attention to the diseases of sex organs. Intermingled with these are communistic and anti-religious slogans and endless statistical tables and cartoons. There are also models of storms of rain and lightning, with their Biblical explanation contrasted with the true meteorological causation. Also ingenious pictures of volcanos, cesspools, etc. Altogether a typical example of stereotyped Russian propaganda. The Five-Year Plan is here illustrated as in the anti-religious and historical museums elsewhere. The club-room is large and clean. A cinema screen is hung above the platform. A grand piano is being loudly and discordantly played, whilst two comrades are playing chess, the others languidly looking on. No cards are played. Vodka and cards apparently go together in this country, and the combination of the two is the worst reproach that can be cast at a worker.

The manager and director harangued us at great length on the virtues and success of Russian agriculture. When asked whether the new collective farms were dirty and choked with weeds, he admitted that one dirty farm contaminated its neighbour, but nevertheless maintained that each peasant succeeds in growing his appointed quota of grain which he sells to the co-operative stores at a price of about 76 kopecks per pood or less. When asked what the price of grain is in the open market, the director did not know, but stoutly denied that it is ever 90 roubles or more, as alleged in Mr. A. C.'s observations.

We sallied forth to-night to try and find a smart Russian restaurant in Moscow. Finally, we pitched on the brightest-looking one, in a large boat moored in the river and hung with hundreds of electric lights. Evidently it had been something very smart in the olden days. It is now shabby and joyless, in spite of its surviving mirrors and paintings. Dirty tablecloths, an excellent orchestra, poor but very dear food and drink. For half a bottle of poor red wine, a fairly good omelette, and two portions of brown bread we paid 32 roubles, according to the prices set forth on the menu. No butter could be got. No tea or coffee. The waiter accepted a tip without comment. Several drunken women and one drunken man sat about the room. One of the customers, an unwashed proletarian, used his fingers in addition to his knife and fork to attack his meal.

All passenger trains, in Moscow as in Leningrad, are packed to overflowing. One sees men, women, and children standing in the floor-space, not only in the cars themselves, but also on the spaces between the cars, and often with the children's legs hanging over the outside.

The Park of Culture and Rest, of which Moscow is specially proud, is a huge amusement park situated on the river bank. We went there one night in a little paddle-boat, crammed as usual to the utmost. The park was brilliantly lit up with festoons of electric lights. The place was thronged, although it was not an official holiday. A good orchestra in one corner was playing classical music to an attentive crowd; elsewhere there were revolving wheels, distorting mirrors, shooting galleries, confectionery booths, a gigantic caricature of a foreign soldier threatening the peaceful Soviet citizen, a circus, a menagerie, and a cinema. We tried to get seats in one of these last, but our foreign money was refused, and so we had to stay outside. In another part of the park folk-dances were being practised by a ring of young teachers under the leadership of a super-expert. These dances were most graceful, with charming poses, occasional rhythmic clapping of hands, and sometimes loud chanting of patriotic refrains. Each of the teachers thus trained proceeds later on to demonstrate the dances to the general public, inviting them to join in, until there are hundreds of people dancing all at once.

The Moscow police, with their tent-like helmets, are posted at street corners on curious wooden platforms about 3 feet high, to supervise the traffic. The effect is sometimes startling, to see an immobile figure gazing fixedly into the distance, like a wax model.

The Kremlin is a large triangular enclosure surrounded by a high red-brick crenellated wall on which are some nineteen towers, dating back to the fifteenth century. Prior to that date there had been an eleventh-century oaken wall. At one time the Kremlin was a younger son's estate, but later it increased in importance and became an imperial fortified city, containing cathedrals, palaces, and barracks. Now it is the headquarters of the Communist government. It has its own hospital.

Napoleon damaged the wall of the Kremlin after his withdrawal, but this was soon repaired. During the 1917 revolution it was again damaged by artillery fire, but all traces of this have been effaced. In the old days its walls were surrounded by a deep moat along which the river Neglinka flowed. This river has long since been diverted underground, and the former moat is now transformed into wooded public gardens.

Each of the nineteen towers has its own name and history. The Spasski gate (Gate of the Saviour) is the main entrance into the Kremlin. Prior to the revolution of 1917, everyone passing through this gate had to uncover his head in homage to the famous picture of the Redeemer standing over the gateway. This picture has now been removed. A drawbridge crosses the moat between the Spasski gate and the Kremlin itself. Within the walls are numerous palaces, cathedrals, and barracks.

The Oruzheinaya Palata, or palace of armour, has been an imperial armoury, and also, since the sixteenth century, a museum. Here are shown treasures belonging to a long line of Tsars, right down to the time of Nicholas II. After the 1917 revolution the treasures from the Patriarch's palace and from various churches and monasteries throughout Russia were added, including many imperial treasures which had been transferred from Petrograd to Moscow at the beginning of the Great War. Within this museum are shown jewelled and embroidered vestments, some of them thickly crusted with pearls, emeralds, and diamonds, also jewelled saddles from Turkish potentates. There is a whole series of gilded state-coaches from various countries, most of them elaborately carved and gilded. One rather plain state-sleigh is almost rectangular in shape, something like a modern railway carriage, and fitted up as a small living-room; this was used to transport one of the Tsarinas from Petersburg to Moscow in the winter-time to be crowned. It was drawn by seventeen horses, and the journey is said to have been accomplished in three days and three nights. All sorts of weapons and armour are shown, also war trophies in ivory, enamel, crystal, and amber. One ivory eagle, larger than life, was presented by the Japanese government on the conclusion of the Russo-Japanese peace in 1906. It is said that if one particular ivory feather be pulled out, the whole bird can be taken to pieces. A curious exhibit is a set of heavy gold chains and a solid gold girdle, dating from the fourth century; these were recently discovered in the possession of peasants, who were using the chains for dog-chains and the rest as playthings. There are gorgeous collections of golden and silver plate. One huge case of silver-gilt flagons and bowls was presented by Elizabeth of England to Boris Goudounoff. Here we see the twelfth-century tent-shaped crown of Vladimir Monomach. The thrones of numerous Tsars, right down to that of Nicholas II, stand here, including the two-seated throne of Peter the Great and his step-brother, the half-witted Ivan, the two of them being crowned together. The whole museum is so crowded with treasures of silver and gold, tapestries, and embroideries that it is difficult to get a separate view of some of them. There is a marble statue of Napoleon, represented as a Roman general, brought to Moscow by Napoleon himself and abandoned when he had to retreat.

Another building within the Kremlin, standing alongside the armoury, is a "Jesters' Theatre," erected by the first of the Romanoff Tsars. Next door to it was a special bath for the theatre-goers, to wash away their sins before going across the street to the cathedral and pray.

In the cathedral square stand several ancient cathedrals. The Cathedral of the Annunciation (*Blagoveschenski Sobor*), with its nine domes, was used for the imperial marriages and baptisms; it is now being carefully restored. The Archangel Cathedral was used for imperial burials, and contains the tombs of the Tsars prior to the time of Peter the

Great, from which time onwards they were buried in Petrograd. This cathedral has recently been restored to its sixteenth-century condition by the removal of successive layers of decorations added by subsequent Tsars. The Cathedral of the Assumption (*Uspenski Sobor*) was used for imperial coronations, and for the burial of patriarchs and metropolitans of the Russian church; it is the largest cathedral of all, dating back to the fifteenth century. Restoration is still going on, and its cupolas are being gilded afresh. Opposite the Uspenski cathedral is the Campanile of Ivan the Great, built by Boris Goudounoff in 1600 to provide relief work during a time of famine. Beside it stand several other bell towers of lesser size. The top of this tower was formerly the highest point in Moscow, but is now exceeded by the tower of the new radio building. The bells of the campanile are hung on bars around the top of the basal part of the structure. The Tsar bell, just outside the cathedral square, is said to be the largest in the world. Originally it was hung under a wooden, tent-shaped roof; in 1738 this caught fire and the bell fell to the ground, breaking off a huge piece from its rim, about 6 feet high, now standing on the ground beside the original bell. The Tsar cannon, a companion-piece to the bell, is much older, having been cast in 1586. As a weapon of war it was useless, although remarkable as a work of art owing to its elaborate sculptured decorations. Several cannon-balls, about 3 feet in diameter, are piled beneath the gun, but they are too large to enter its mouth.

We had not the necessary permits of admission to the great Palace of the Kremlin with the White Hall of St. George, nor to the Granitovaya Palata, where the imperial Crown jewels are kept.

The Boyar's House in Moscow is a beautiful little seventeenth-century mansion, where the boyar, Michael Feodorovitch, the first Romanoff Tsar, once lived. It has been carefully preserved with its original furniture and decorations. A long flight of stone steps, flanked by red stone lions at the bottom, leads up to the ground-floor, the house being built on a steep slope. The main living-room has an arched and vaulted ceiling, highly decorated. It has small windows with panes of mica. The seventeenth-century furniture includes a sort of refectory table, at the head of which the boyar sat in a snug arm-chair. There are gold and silver goblets, a golden loving-cup, and a stoneware wine-keg. The boyar's private study still has one of his own primitive MSS. on the table, whilst his steel treasure-box has a sloping lid, so that it could be slipped under his pillow at night. His steel helmet and chain-mail corselet are in excellent preservation. On the wall hangs an English engraving of Potemkin, the first Russian ambassador to the English court in 1682. In the bedroom stands a four-poster bed with rich tapestry hangings. A small private chapel contains a *prie-dieu*, and on its wall hang beautiful old ikons, one of St. George and another of St. Antipi, who specialized in the cure of toothache. There is an ikon of another saint who presided over war, whilst his neighbouring saint looked after maternity cases. There is a holy-water brush in the corner. A steep, narrow staircase, with a silken rope balustrade, leads up to a series of small rooms now filled with pictures, models, and posters illustrating the downtrodden state of women in the middle ages, their useless luxury under modern capitalism, and their entire freedom under Soviet government. There is an amusing picture of Pharaoh's daughter, in a seventeenth-century costume with a long cylindrical fur hat, stooping to lift the infant Moses from a wicker basket. Alongside this is a recent photograph from the U.S.A. showing a woman communist leader being arrested for leading a procession; also pictures of rich Americans in a crowded restaurant, whilst poverty-stricken Americans form a food queue in the street outside.

We visited the Institute of Industrial Diseases, which is under the direction of a lady doctor, Mme Bogolepova. This Institute was established in 1923 following a series of severe epidemics which had decimated the population of Moscow. It is the first of its kind in Russia. The assistant director received us courteously, and explained the various departments which make up the Institute. There is a clinical division or hospital, with about one hundred and fifty beds, under various specialists, medical, surgical, neuro-pathological, dermatological, etc. There is also a polyclinic for out-patients transferred from other hospitals for consultation. There are special departments for the study of industrial diseases peculiar to the metallurgical, agricultural, mining, and other industries. There is also a prophylactic clinic for the study and treatment of patients who are recovering from various maladies so as to establish at what period, if any, they become fit for work, and if unfit, what work they are still capable of doing. Some of these patients go to work in the daytime and return to the clinic to sleep the night. (We had seen a similar night-home in Leningrad.) The medical staff consists of two hundred men and women, including thirty or forty non-medical laboratory and scientific workers. There are well-equipped laboratories, clinical, anatomical, physiological, cardiological, basal metabolic, physiological (under the eminent professor Raziankoff), hygienic, electro-therapeutic, radiological, etc. In addition to research work in the medical and surgical treatment of occupational maladies, post-graduate lectures are given by the various experts on the staff. There is a medical and scientific library of some sixteen thousand volumes.

Professor Gelman, chief of the medical division, told us of his recent observations on a series of cases of pseudo-uraemia. This is a malady occurring in workers constantly exposed to high temperatures which induce copious sweating with excessive elimination of NaCl. For example, a worker whose habitual solid diet consisted of bread, salt, and herring, forgot his salt for one day. He promptly developed dangerous pseudo-uraemic symptoms, including coma, convulsions, feeble heart, and low blood-pressure. There was no excess of urea in the blood, and no albuminuria. NaCl was deficient both in the urine and in the blood. Treatment consisted in intra-venous injections of hypertonic (30 per cent) solution for several successive days. No patient of the series has died. The symptoms can be prevented by making the worker drink, not ordinary water, but water containing salt to half the strength of normal saline solution.

Professor Gelman also related to us some of his researches on the subject of the causation of relapses in rheumatic fever. He regards this malady as an infective one, but with a personal bodily reaction, which determines the type and severity of the symptoms. Relapses can sometimes be foretold by observing an excessively rapid sedimentation of the red cells in the blood, and by the presence of an excess of fibrinogen, 6 to 8 per cent, instead of the normal 2 to 4 per cent. Preventive treatment is being tried by the use of $CaCl_2$ (10 c.cm. of a 5 per cent solution) intravenously for five or six days. Also treatment by auto-haemotherapy is being used.

We learned, by questioning the assistant director, something of the present economic conditions for medical men in Soviet Russia. Every medical man or woman is a State official. Nearly every medical officer is attached to a local panel of patients in his district. Patients attend as ambulatory cases at the public dispensary to which their particular medical man is attached. Bedridden patients, if not transferred to hospitals or other public institutions, are attended by their local doctor, who must go on foot or by tram. Specially urgent cases, however, are dealt with by a special urgency-doctor, for whom a special official car is available. Every patient has the right to telephone for urgent medical help; if the case proves after all to be trivial, so that the summons was unnecessary, a suitable financial penalty is exacted. Every doctor must work five hours a day. For this the standard rate of wages is 250 roubles a month. For extra work, or by taking on two separate billets, extra pay can be earned, up to about 500 roubles. Eminent men, with specially responsible posts, may, in rare cases, earn up to 1,500 or even 2,000 roubles a month. Nearly all patients are treated free of charge. There is little or no private practice, but for such as there is, the doctor may keep the extra fees. The standard consultant fee is 25 roubles. No extra fee is charged for surgical operations. Scientific men who write articles for publication are paid at the rate of 300 roubles per sixteen pages. Lectures are also paid extra.

With these meagre conditions Russian doctors seem to be satisfied: at any rate, they make no complaint. They are allotted two or three rooms, with a certain minimum of cubic space, for themselves and families. Even in a house which may have been the doctor's private property in pre-revolutionary days, no more than three rooms are allowed to him. The remainder are shared out between other workers. Compared with pre-war times, the incomes of the leading physicians and surgeons have sunk to a fraction of their previous earnings. Nevertheless they are, ostensibly, philosophical and uncomplaining. The rank and file of medical practitioners appear to be a little worse off than before. At the age of sixty a medical man has the right, if he so desires, to retire on a pension, at the rate of 50 per cent of his wages. On the other hand, he is still permitted to supplement his salary by continuing to work, either as a part-time or whole-time worker. Thus the whole medical profession has become an organized State service.

The Dyetskoi theatre (Theatre of Youth) is a large building, holding perhaps a thousand people. When we went one evening every seat was occupied by the usual crowd of workers. No smoking was allowed. The stage had no drop-curtain, and all the scene-shifting was done in view of the audience on the darkened stage during the *entr'actes*. There was a revolving stage with three "sets," one for each act, accessory properties being fixed by hammering on to the surrounding fixed platform. The background, above the level of the action, consisted of a series of horizontal white screens, forming zig-zag angles projecting into the main scenery. Below these screens effects of distance were cleverly achieved. In one scene, representing the bridge of a battleship, the platform with its machine-guns projected through the upper row of these white screens. The stage was first violently illuminated by rapidly revolving flashlights. Then a steady illumination was turned on, and the plot proceeded. It was a propagandist play, illustrating the dissipated and extravagant lives of foreign naval officers, who spent their time dancing and drinking, contrasted with the stern asceticism of the patriotic Red Fleet. Several comic scenes were introduced, showing life in a naval port, with a Carmen singing, dancing, and having drunken orgies with two Russian sailors, also the subsequent repentance of these two, and their trial before a soviet of their comrades. Finally, there was a battle scene ashore, in which the Moscow radio announced to the advance-guard in the trenches that the western front had been invaded. The detachment of G.P.U. guards, in their characteristic green caps, was now reinforced by a volunteer party of sailors, hurried across from the battleship. This combined party defended the trench with rifle and machine-gun fire, directed straight at the audience. They were killed to the last man. One dying hero achieved a sensational dramatic effect by dragging himself to a blackboard at one end of the trench and writing on it the legend 162,000,000, representing the population of Russia. He then wrote underneath it the figure 27, representing the advance guard killed by the enemy. With increasing difficulty he succeeded in writing beneath this the figure 161,000,973, representing the number of Soviet Russians still surviving and prepared to fight to the death. Finally, he called upon every member of the audience belonging to the Red Army or to the Communist Party to stand up. About half of the assembly, men and women, stood up, cheering loudly. The incident was striking, and illustrated the ceaseless propaganda by means of which Russians are taught to expect war. Cinema films of the Russian navy, army, and air force, including one showing Voroshiloff, the Commissar for War, evoked great enthusiasm, being interspersed between the acting scenes. One comic film without political significance was also shown.

The theatre seats were comfortable, tip-up, wooden affairs. The price of ours was 6 roubles. Factory workers, who buy them in large batches, get a discount of about 45 per cent. During the *entr'actes* a large part of the audience adjourned into a tightly packed foyer with buffets at which a pink, strawberry-flavoured water was sold in bottles, together with a few fancy cakes. Nothing alcoholic was served, and there was no smoking.

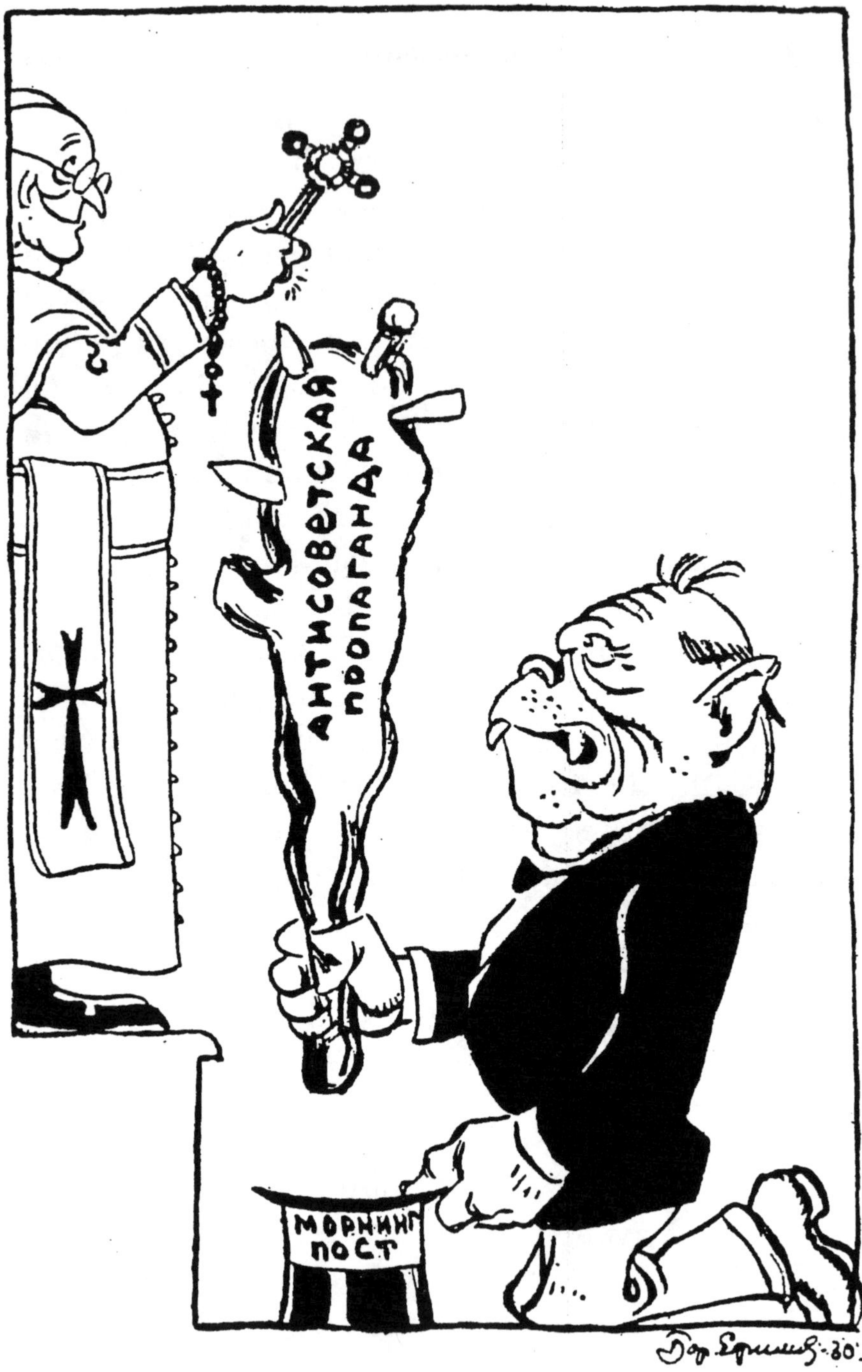

THE HOLY FATHER AND HIS HOLY SON

The Editor of the *Morning Post*, with his anti-soviet propaganda bludgeon, receiving a special blessing from the Pope of Rome

August 26th

The PRISON, OR CORRECTIONAL COLONY, of Levortovski, was formerly a military prison with 205 cells for solitary confinement. The cells are arranged in four long galleries, each of three storeys, radiating from a centre. It now houses 615 prisoners, three in a cell. This particular "colony" has been running for two years. Since the Revolution ten prisons in Moscow have been demolished and never rebuilt. This is one reason why the present prisons are so crowded. In this colony only male prisoners are admitted. Most of them are first offenders; a few are recidivists. The chief crimes for which "treatment" is given are robbery with violence, theft, embezzlement, rape, and murder. The maximum penalty, even for murder, is ten years. The only crimes for which the death penalty is now exacted are (1) counter-revolutionary activities, (2) organized murders by bands of criminals, and (3) group raping, an offence rarely heard of outside Russia. Seldom does a murderer on the expiry of his "treatment" commit a second murder; if he does, he is executed. Educated prisoners receive heavier sentences than illiterate ones.

Each cell is fitted with a radio loud-speaker above its door. The beds are clean and comfortable. The barred windows are large. The doors of the cells are left wide open, except between 1 a.m. and 6 a.m., so that prisoners can visit each other freely. One cell, which we passed, had been padlocked on the outside by the prisoner himself. Presently he turned up, opened the padlock, and welcomed us to his cell. He was a stout elderly gentleman, who informed us that he had been sentenced to ten years' confinement for embezzlement of 71,000 roubles from a sugar trust. He is leaving to-day in high spirits, having, by his industry and good conduct, served exactly six years, ten months, and fifty-seven days. He told us that he has secured a secretarial post in the office of the Commissary of Trade at a salary of 700 roubles a month, and will take up his new duties forthwith.

Meals are served to the prisoners in their cells, but a comfortable communal dining-room will presently be built. Each prisoner is expected to work eight hours a day, knocking off for a meal. There are two separate shifts of workers. If he is illiterate, this defect must be "liquidated," and he must learn to read and write, being instructed by fellow-prisoners who were teachers in civil life. Non-illiterate prisoners are employed in one or other of the various prison factories, chiefly in spinning, weaving, tailoring, and embroidering. For this work the pay is from 30 to 35 roubles a month. This amount is placed to each man's account, to be handed to him on leaving. He is allowed to spend a certain proportion on clothes, tobacco, etc., but not on alcohol. He has a week's holiday in his own home after one year; this is increased to a fortnight in subsequent years, and if he is a peasant he may be allowed to stay at home for three months to help in getting in the harvest. His friends and family can come and visit him in prison, every ten days during the first year and every five days in subsequent years. No prison uniform is worn. The outside guards are armed, but the inner guards are elected from amongst the prisoners themselves, who have a local soviet which inflicts suitable punishments on prisoners who offend their fellow-men. This soviet also controls the inside warders and prison officials, and even suggests amendments in the prison regulations. There is a dramatic society, a chess club, a drawing class, a musical circle, technical classes in engineering, etc., and a library of six thousand books dealing with historical, technical, and general literature, also romance. The librarian, a delicate-looking man of twenty-three, is serving a two years' sentence for a sexual offence which he was too shy to explain, beyond mentioning that it falls under Section 182 of the criminal code. There is an excellent theatre which was formerly the prison chapel. In the old days each prisoner attended service by entering a separate partitioned box, with a small peep-hole through which he could see the priest. These partitions have all been demolished.

Each work-day performed by the prisoner cuts more than a day off his sentence, two days' work corresponding to three days' remission of prison. A "communistic week" is worked, i.e. five days' work and one day's rest. Reluctant or lazy prisoners are tried by their fellow-prisoners and deprived of their holidays, visitors, entertainments, and other privileges. There are ordinary baths and Turkish baths. I saw the barber's shop in one cell, with several customers being beautified. The prices are 20 kopecks for a shave, 30 kopecks for hair-cut, 45 kopecks for shampoo, 30 kopecks for eau-de-Cologne spray, and 60 kopecks for a complete shaving of the whole head. A close hair-cut with clippers, i.e. "a prison crop," is free. Within the building are a dispensary and hospital, under the charge of a doctor (non-prisoner) and a woman nurse-attendant. The hospital kitchen is under the charge of a picturesque, happy old man with long whiskers and enormous moustaches, which he takes a special pride in twisting round his ears. He is serving a ten years' sentence for having murdered his wife owing to jealousy. The dentist's operating-room is housed in what used to be the black cell, now excellently lit by large windows. Propagandist posters line all the public rooms and most of the cells; there are also illustrated wall-newspapers, written by the prisoners themselves. Homosexuality is frequent amongst the inmates. It is not considered as a criminal offence, and is treated by persuasion and teaching.

I inquired from a series of prisoners what their crimes had been, and their sentences, with the following results:

Embezzlement of government funds—one-and-a-half years.

Rape—three years (a young man of vacant and sub-normal mentality)

Misappropriation of 1,500 roubles from the funds of a collective farm, when acting as chairman —two-and-a-half years.

Embezzlement of building funds—two-and-a-half years.

Private selling of collective farm grain—three years.

Working under an assumed name—three years.

Theft of coat from a fellow worker—two years.

Refusal to perform military service—two years. This prisoner was a Baptist and a conscientious objector.

We were informed that no prisoner has ever attempted to escape from this prison. In view of the numerous social amenities here enjoyed, in contrast with the hardships of the ordinary worker's life, this is perhaps not to be wondered at.

An interesting sidelight on human life in Russia and the penalty for its destruction is recorded in yesterday's *Moscow News.* The door-keeper of a block of workers' flats killed his wife during an alcoholic outburst. The incident was duly reported to the local soviet for adjudication. It was decided that inasmuch as the man was drunk at the time when he committed the offence, he was not responsible for his action. Accordingly he was reprimanded and transferred as door-keeper to a different block of flats.

CHAPTER IV

THE VOLGA

August 27th

AFTER an all-night train journey from Moscow we reached Nizhni-Novgorod this morning on a cold but sunny day. Several officers of the Red army, talking nothing but Russian, travelled in our carriage, and we made friends with them. One of the fiercest looking was Dmitri Ivanovitch, a cavalry officer, wearing two Mohammedan star-shaped decorations on his tunic. These he had gained in successive campaigns around Bokhara in 1917 and 1922. He also wore a smaller Red decoration for excellence in physical culture. He was a very nice fellow, travelling on his annual leave of absence down the Volga to Astrakan. All the expenses of this official holiday are defrayed by the government.

At one of the stations, where we stopped a while, crammed as usual with peasants waiting for the next train (ours was full up) stood an ancient chapel of white-painted brick. Its windows were broken, its doors padlocked, and a placard announced that it is now a *masterskaya*, or workshop.

Nizhni-Novgorod was formerly the site of the world-famous annual fair. Since the Revolution it has become dingy, dilapidated and dirty, and the fair is a thing of the past. Merchants no longer come from the Far East. Private trading is illegal, and they must now sell their goods to the government co-operative stores. The main city is situated on the high right bank of the Volga, just below its confluence with the smaller Oka river. On the high ground, which forms the right bank of the Volga throughout its course, stands a thirteenth-century Kremlin, with red-brick towers and crenellated battlements. Inside this is a beautiful thirteenth-century cathedral with a gilded cupola. Outside the Kremlin, in the modern public square, stands a massive marble pedestal surmounted by an incongruous electric-light standard. Here formerly stood a statue of Alexander II. The statue has been demolished, and the inscriptions around the pedestal roughly chipped off. The former merchants' quarter, where the great fair was held, was situated on the low flat ground on the opposite bank, usually flooded every spring. Here one sees twelve or fourteen long parallel rows of barrack-like sheds. These formerly housed the merchants and their goods, but are now deserted and decaying. The wooden bridge from this quarter across the Oka is being replaced by a huge new bridge of steel and stone.[1] The streets, both of the city on the high ground and of the low-lying merchant quarter, paved with cobblestones, are in bad repair, in-

[1] A month later we read in the papers that a huge steel span of this bridge crashed from its supports into the river, drowning or injuring scores of workers.

credibly rough and dirty. A few dingy stores and shops occupy what used to be prosperous business premises.

We stayed only a short time in Nizhni and were quickly shepherded on board a large passenger steamer, *Parizheskaya Communa*, for a four days' voyage down the Volga. This ship possesses several tiers of decks with promenades, an airy saloon, plain but clean cabins, and filthy sanitary accommodation, despite the abundance of running water. "Workers" on the lower decks are huddled into open wooden cages, stacked in layers.

The right bank of the Volga is steep nearly all the way, whilst its left bank is flat and usually flooded in the spring-time. Consequently most of the important Volga towns are situated on its right bank. Eighty-four kilometres below Nizhni, on the left bank of the Volga, is the huge walled monastery of Makarieff, looking almost like a walled town with its nine churches and cathedral, its gilded domes and white towers glittering in the afternoon sun.

The Volga, although magnificently wide, has many shallows and sandbanks, so that big ships, like our own, have to steer a tortuous course, the channel being marked out by occasional buoys. These are illuminated at night by a lamp-lighter, who rows out from the bank to mark out his own stretch of river by hanging oil-lamps on the hooks attached to the tops of these buoys. At every stopping-stage crowds of peasants embarked and disembarked.

August 28th

We arrived at Kazan, four hours late. Consequently all the sightseeing which we had projected was reduced to a tram-ride to the city, situated on a hill two miles inland, and back again. About a mile from home, on the return journey, the electrical power gave out. We had to walk the rest, and nearly missed our boat.

Kazan is now a dilapidated and shabby country town, which in pre-revolutionary days must have been beautiful, with its spires, domes, and minarets. Our guide alleges that it now possesses fifteen universities and one hundred and fifty schools. I doubt this. At the former Imperial University of Kazan, Leo Tolstoy, Lenin, and other Russian notabilities were students. The university has now been renamed the Ulianov–Lenin State University. We only saw it from a distance. There is a red-brick Kremlin with white crenellated walls encompassing the old Tartar town and its seven-storey Sumbeck Tower. This was built by an ancient Khan of Tartary to seclude his beautiful daughter from the wiles of her Russian lover. In the fields outside the town walls lie rafts of logs, high and dry, the remnant of a much larger quantity floated down the river Kazanka to join the Volga. In spring-time the Kazanka swells into a vast stream, up which even great Volga steamers can come. Now in summer-time it is a small river, running at the bottom of a muddy ravine, about 15 or 20 feet below the level of the stranded logs which once floated on its surface. A curious pyramidal building in the fields, with white pillars on each side, is a monument erected in 1823 to the memory of the heroes who fell in the battle of 1552, when Kazan was captured by Ivan the Terrible. When the Kazanka is in flood, this monument becomes an island in the stream and its base is submerged, just like Phylæ in the Nile.

During 1918 Kazan was in possession of the Czecho-slovak troops for a month. They then retreated before the Red forces, wisely taking with them the huge Russian gold reserve which had been placed in the State Bank here for safety. There are said to be sixty churches and six mosques in the city. Only two of the churches are now in use, and neither of the mosques. Nearly all the inhabitants, whether Russian Orthodox believers or Mohammedans, now pride themselves on being *bezbozhniki*, i.e. atheists. Religion throughout the U.S.S.R. is regarded as a pre-revolutionary superstition.

The porters at the Volga landing-stages are able to carry enormous loads on their backs, a whole packing-case at a time. This is achieved by the help of a curious shelf-like saddle, suspended from the shoulders and resting on the lumbo-sacral vertebrae. A small ridge at the free edge of this shelf prevents the load from slipping off. Even the women can shoulder huge weights. One in particular, with an enormous sack of goods slung over her back, stopped at the landing-stage to have her brown boots brightly polished.

August 29th

We are sailing down the ever-winding Volga, with villages, lime-kilns, and windmills scattered along its banks. The river forms a steep loop around the Zheguli mountains which project inwards from the western bank, causing the Volga to make a great sigmoid bend, more than a hundred miles long, called the Samara Bend, instead of the twelve miles which it would otherwise have followed, had it run straight.

SAMARA, the great grain city of the Volga, is built on a series of terraces on the left bank. Amongst the trees on the river-bank above the city we see many large and beautiful country houses of modern construction, with graceful staircases and statuary. These are now "homes of rest" for the workers. All of them fly the Soviet red flag. Farther down the river the environs of the city are occupied by closely huddled wooden shacks. On the topmost height of the city itself several huge new rectangular buildings of cubist style are nearing completion, apparently workers' dwellings.

Samara itself is dirty and dilapidated. Its main street, cobble-paved, is adorned at one end by the inevitable statue of Lenin. Our guide, a swarthy Ukrainian, informed us that all the churches in the city, except two, are being utilized for other purposes. In the main street we saw the German church, now an anti-religious museum. The Polish cathedral, with graceful hollow spires, is now a cinema and theatrical school. Another church which we passed has been razed to the ground-level and on its old foundations a workers' club is being built.

At the entrance to an alley opening off the main street a large brown-paper placard was stuck on the wall, stating: "Here lives the idle Tshedoff, who does not do his work and hinders others from working." If Tshedoff were to tear this down (it has been posted up by his fellow-workers) he would be arrested and punished, and a notice of the affair would be published in the local press.

I met an American–Russian engineer from New York who, being out of work in New York, took a job here eight months ago under the government as an automobile and tractor constructor. His fare here was paid. He receives 400 roubles a month, with rooms for himself and his wife. At the end of his two-year contract he must either become a Russian citizen or be deported back to the U.S.A. He may not take any Russian roubles out of the country; there is, therefore, no object in saving. His American money he has already spent in the Torgsin stores, which only accept foreign currency. To me his prospects seem far from rosy, but he seems fairly satisfied, or perhaps resigned.

August 30th

We got off the boat for half an hour at a little town called VOLSK. The usual crowd of shabby hawkers lined the roadside from the landing-stage. Three little dried brown fishes, about the size of whiting, were 1.50 roubles. A small chicken, ready cooked, was 10 roubles. A melon cost 1.20 roubles.

The large town square has a beautiful pre-revolutionary white building on one side, with graceful corinthian pillars, in sharp contrast with the remaining dingy and decaying buildings, now occupied by co-operative stores of various sorts. The workers, however, who thronged the square and the landing stage, seemed comfortably dressed and well nourished.

We are now eight hours behind our scheduled time on the steamer trip, so that our prospects of seeing Sarátoff in daylight are very dim.

SARÁTOFF, the biggest town on the Volga, was reached after sundown. Our view of it and its night life was therefore short and scanty. It is the busiest town we have seen since Moscow. Its streets are thronged with young people; there are cinemas, theatres, and a park of "culture and rest," all doing a roaring trade.

August 31st

Below Sarátoff the river passes through the so-called Volga–German Republic. This region has been successfully cultivated by German colonists since the time of Catherine the Great, herself a German princess. The German standard of agriculture was always higher than the Russian. Prior to the revolution of 1917 this countryside was highly prosperous and contented. After the revolution some of these Germans escaped to Germany. The remainder struggled on, under increasing difficulties, but even in 1925, according to our official Soviet guide-book, the proportion of Germans in the Republic was still as high as 64 per cent. In 1929, owing to the severity with which the government proceeded to "liquidate the kulaks," i.e. to stamp out private farmers and forced them into the collective farms by exacting an excessive quota of grain and by a crushing taxation, thousands of German farmers and their families, both from this district and from other parts of Russia, journeyed to Moscow. There they camped, in and around the empty cottages near the city, demanding permission to be repatriated to Germany. The Soviet Government ostensibly described this movement as that of a religious sect, the Mennonites, although many other varieties of Protestant creed were included amongst them. The true reason for their attempted return to Germany was not merely religious persecution but the economic ruin of these formerly prosperous farmers. Only a few of them succeeded in struggling back to Germany; the rest were deported to Siberia.

CHAPTER V

STALINGRAD. ROSTOFF. KHARKOFF. KIEFF. WARSAW

September 1st

Last night, after sunset, we reached STALINGRAD. Most of our S.C.R. party, after a hurried and dusty drive around the town in pitch darkness, decided to travel on at once to Rostoff. F. G. and I arranged to wait and see Stalingrad by daylight.

To-day we had our breakfast and other meals in the restaurant of "The Park of Culture and Rest." Walking to this, through the public gardens, where a little perfunctory weeding was being carried out by girl workers, a loud-speaker from an adjacent public building filled the air with piano music.

Stalingrad is a big city whose population within the last few years has grown from 80,000 to 480,000. It has been specially developed because of its proximity to the proposed Don-Volga canal which will carry its manufactured products westward. This canal, however, has not yet been begun.

The town itself is dusty and dilapidated, reminding us rather of Bloemfontein, which both of us had seen in war-time. The roads are deplorable and full of enormous pot-holes. Here and there, however, gangs of men and women labourers are building stretches of *chaussée* paved with rough stone setts. In the largest public square, a huge pile of red-brick rubbish, about 40 feet high, is all that remains of the Cathedral which has been blown up to make place for a new pile of government offices.

Malaria and enteric fever are endemic in the town, which is ice-bound in winter, ankle-deep in dust in the summer, and swampy in the spring. Its streets show curiously contrasting pictures: bullock-wagons, camels, and electric tramways. Aeroplanes fly over the city. Two little girls of about six carry a tiny bier with the body of a new-born baby, its little face covered with muslin, and bunches of red flowers arranged around it; no procession follows.

We drove out from the city for about ten miles to visit the great tractor works named after the sinister Djerjinsky. On the way out we passed the "Red October" steel-mills with huge blocks of new workers' dwellings growing up apace. A large domed church is now a workers' club. Cartoons at the factory gates show how cattle on every farm will in the future be displaced by tractors. Amongst the factory buildings fire-engine stations are posted here and there, each with its watchman perched on a tall, look-out tower. This is a wise precaution, in view of the old wooden buildings in which many of the workers live.

In front of the main building of the great Djerjinsky tractor-works is a large open square. In the centre of this a small platform for public speakers has been erected, on a curious spirally ascending base, supposed to represent the spirit of mechanization.

This factory has been in action since June 1930, just over two years. Its proposed output of tractors is given as 50,000 a year, i.e. over 4,000 a month. During the first five months of the present year the successive monthly outputs have been, 2,825, 2,883, 2,700, 2,991, and 1,897, i.e. an average of 2,655 per month, as posted up in their own wall-newspaper. At present things are being specially delayed because of the absence of radiators and magnetos, which have to be manufactured in Leningrad.

The tractor-factory, which we went through, is a grandoise affair. We saw castings being moulded in sand and then cast, the plant where steel parts are forged, struck, and case-hardened, also the mighty steel hammers, where white-hot bars of steel are pounded into moulds, and so on. We also saw the "assembly buildings" where the bare chassis is carried along a slowly moving belt, having a fresh part added to it every few yards until it finally emerges, painted, varnished, and ready to be driven off as soon as petrol is poured into the tank. As a matter of fact, however, this did not happen, owing to the temporary absence of magnetos and radiators. Nevertheless the works are impressive. The whole organization and equipment were bought in America, and a large number of American engineers and technicians came across to set things going. Mr. R. S., however, who had talked with one of these American technicians yesterday, tells me that 90 per cent of the Americans have recently left, owing to their pay having been changed over from a dollar to a rouble basis.

Unskilled workers, of whom there seems to be more than enough, are permitted to migrate from factory to factory, but skilled workers, no matter how dissatisfied they may be, are "discouraged" from leaving a factory where they are needed. Pressure is exerted upon them by their trade unions, which have the power of withdrawing certain privileges. The director of this factory has a monthly salary of 1,800 roubles, the superintendents of divisions get 800, technicians 500. Some of the skilled workers, e.g. hammer-men who manipulate the gigantic steam hammers, get as much as 700 roubles a month.

The workers' club of the Djerjinsky factory is a new and well-built structure. In its large entrance-hall, in addition to the usual portraits, slogans, and red banners, hangs a wall-newspaper containing not only political news but five or six photographs of workers in the factory who have recently distinguished themselves by special industry. There is the usual graph or curve, indicating a continuous rise in factory output, a continuity which their own figures fail to substantiate (*vide supra*). There are excellent reading-rooms, study-rooms, class-rooms, lecture-rooms, rest-rooms, and a fine gymnasium with a gallery. On the wall of one of the halls hangs a large oil-painting with a spirited representation of a group of Chinese Red soldiers.

The factory village also has a circus, a dispensary, a primary school, a technical school, a "university" for technical instruction, and a large hotel for visitors.

The dispensary has been open since November 1931, i.e. less than a year. It is a large two-storey building with a frontage of twenty-two windows. It is not yet completely equipped. Nevertheless it already possesses surgical, medical, gynaecological, X-ray, electro-therapeutical, and other divisions, each under the charge of a couple of hospital sisters. The department for nervous diseases is a sub-section of the massage department.

The medical superintendent, a young man of about 35, clad in a grey shirt and pants, informed me that there are 80 beds in the dispensary, for which they have 83 qualified medical officers—rather an excessive staff. They see 2,000 patients daily. The population of the works is about 35,000, of whom 12,000 are workers, 4,000 technicians, and the remaining 19,000, wives, families, and etceteras. The government pays 10 per cent of each worker's wages for medical services (this is not deducted from his wages). A sick worker receives full pay for the first four months of his illness, and all treatment, medicinal or dietetic, is provided free.

Information as to the economic position of doctors

corroborates what we were told in Moscow. Thus the pay of these dispensary doctors varies from 220 to 350 roubles, working 5 hours daily. Most of them hold two separate billets, in different clinics, etc., so as to supplement their income up to about 500 roubles. Each medical man is a "specialist" in some department. The young administrator who showed us round specialized as a neurologist. From his income 1 per cent is deducted as government tax, and 2 per cent for trade-union dues. Every "honest" citizen is also expected to subscribe at least three weeks' wages per annum to the various government loans, some yielding interest, others not. These the investor is not allowed to sell, without obtaining special leave from a committee. The rent of one room for a single man comes to 5.60 roubles; for a small flat of three rooms, suitable for man, wife, and child, the monthly rent is 45 roubles. Meals are taken in a communal dining-room, in company with the factory technicians. Here the food, which is better in quality than that of the ordinary factory-workers, costs 3 or 3½ roubles a day, i.e. 90 or 100 roubles a month. A coarse suit of clothes from the co-operative store costs 60 roubles, and boots 18 roubles. If an extra suit of clothes is desired, in addition to his regular allowance, this costs a great deal more than the co-operative price, being regarded as a luxury and not a necessity.

The Seventh Soviet Hospital of Stalingrad, one of nine district hospitals in the city, is a new building of 250 beds, situated on a hill. The road from the railway at the foot is horribly rough, and one pities the unfortunate patients, if they are seriously ill, who must reach the hospital by ambulance. This is a general hospital, staffed by 13 medical officers and 35 nursing-sisters. The sisters vary in their degree of training. Some have only attended a Red Cross dispensary. This scanty personnel contrasts with the 83 medical officers at the factory dispensary of 80 beds for minor ailments. Of the 13 medical men, two are resident in the hospital, the others visit daily, five days out of six, to do their 5½ hours' duty.

There are general medical and surgical wards, a maternity ward, a gynaecological and abortion department, and five operating-theatres. The wards are clean and bright, but the beds are more closely packed than we would sanction in England. All maternity cases in the district come into hospital for accouchement; none are delivered in their own homes. No general anaesthetics are used during labour. There has been no fatal case here in a series of 2,000 deliveries. The abortion clinic carries out 1,000 cases every year, the patients obtaining admission only on the recommendation of a doctor. There is a small clinical laboratory for doing serological and other tests. There is no mortuary and no pathologist. Post-mortem examinations are scanty, 20 to 25 a year, and are carried out by the medical officer who has had clinical charge of the patient in question. The beds of the hospital are never so full as to require a waiting-list. Infectious diseases are treated in a special hospital, a short distance away.

Two ambulance cars are at the disposal of the hospital for the conveyance of patients. Each factory also possesses its own ambulance.

The monthly salary of the head medical officer is 300 roubles. But he, like most of his colleagues, also works in a second clinic elsewhere, making his wages up to a total of 500 roubles. The other medical officers in the hospital receive from 220 to 240 roubles. Several of them are married, always to workers, often to women-doctors, who practise medicine like themselves; others to wives who work as secretaries, teachers, journalists, etc.

In the case of a doctor earning 300 roubles a month, if living alone, he pays a government tax of 6.50 roubles, i.e. $2\frac{1}{4}$ per cent. If he has a wife and child, his tax is reduced to 5.20 roubles. For an unmarried doctor earning 600 roubles, the Government tax is 25 roubles, i.e. over 4 per cent, whereas if married he only pays 8.90 roubles. Medical officers have meals in a communal dining-hall for technicians and doctors, at a daily cost of 3 to $3\frac{1}{2}$ roubles, i.e. about 100 roubles a month. Rent comes to about 14 roubles a month.

Pensions are available, but information on this point is scanty. Few doctors, under the present régime, have reached pensionable age, which is stated at 50 to 55 years, when the medical officer is entitled to retire on an income varying from 50 per cent of his salary downwards, according to his length of service. He need not retire, however, unless he so wishes, but can either go on working as before, or draw his pension and do part-time work to supplement it. The number of medical men throughout Russia is obviously far too small for the work required from them. This is partly due to the greater attractiveness and higher pay of other "technical" professions, such as engineering. Consequently the medical profession does not attract the best type of man, compared with some other countries. Women-doctors, however, are increasing in numbers.

The life of a country doctor in a village, drawing a salary of 200 roubles, is really cheaper as regards living expenses. Often the village community adds another 100 roubles to his official wage. Like his city brother, he only needs to work five hours a day. He usually has an unqualified or partially trained assistant, who helps him on the five ordinary working days and takes entire charge on the sixth or rest-day. He has a month's holiday in the year, a *locum tenens* being provided by the government.

Each citizen in a district belongs to the free panel of his district doctor. If he wishes to be examined or treated by another doctor of his own choice, he can arrange this by paying the non-district doctor out of his own pocket. But there is little or no private practice, except for a few leading specialists in the great university towns, who are allowed to charge a consulting-fee up to 25 roubles.

September 2nd

We left Stalingrad just before midnight, our party now being reduced to our two selves. The railway journey to Rostoff took nearly all day, the first half being specially slow and tedious, lumbering along a single-line railway at a speed of less than twenty miles an hour and stopping at innumerable little stations. The countryside was an open rolling plain, dotted with farms, on which cattle and an occasional camel graze. At every stopping-place there was a hurried rush of train passengers to buy foodstuffs from the village hawkers lying in wait, selling melons, cooked chickens, sausages, sun-flower seeds, slices of dry black bread, meat patties, and eggs.

In the evening we passed a large military camp. Several battalions of Red infantry were drilling. At one side of the huge parade-ground was a large red-painted platform, from which an orator could harangue the troops. A park of artillery was encamped farther on; the men being housed in large pyramidal marquees, much larger than our army bell-tents at home, and accommodating, to look at them, about 50 or 60 men apiece.

At one or two railway-stations, old men tottered along the platform, begging for food or a few coppers. These beggars were incredibly ragged and filthy, much more miserable than any seen in Western countries, with clothes hanging about them like leaves, old straw-plaited shoes on their feet, and their ankles swathed in odd scraps of cloth or felt, held together by string.

September 3rd

ROSTOFF is a big bustling city, with broad well-paved boulevards, flanked by the usual shabby government shops, large and small. A young Austrian chemist, employed as an expert in one of the factories, talked with me at breakfast this morning. He has a contract under which he makes a salary of 1,300 to 1,500 roubles per month. It costs him 1,000 roubles to live comfortably in the hotel. Being a foreign specialist, he is exceptionally well off, so long as he remains in the country. But when he comes to leave, he knows he can neither take his roubles out of Russia nor exchange them for foreign valuta. This drawback is not divulged to foreign specialists when they enter, consequently when they realize that there is no future for them, except as Russian citizens, they hasten to leave the country as soon as their contracts expire. This particular specialist thinks that of all the specialist professions in Russia, doctors are by far the worst paid; hence the increasing scarcity of men doctors and the rising proportion of women in the profession.

Driving round the city we saw the great Paulovski church in process of demolition. The Armenian quarter of Rostoff still possesses one fine old church in use as such. This faces across a public square in which stands a statue of Karl Marx, mounted on a pedestal which originally supported a statue of Catherine the Great. The former bronze decorations and inscriptions have been stripped off and replaced by suitable communistic sentiments.

Rostoff contains the great "Selmarsh" factory for agricultural implements, installed on the American plan, like the Djerjinski works in Stalingrad. There is the usual modern workers' village around the factory. We visited a couple of workers' dwellings in these modern buildings. One flat had two rooms and a bathroom, with electric light and water laid on, sharing a communal kitchen with the other inhabitants on the same floor. In these two rooms six people lived. The rent was 22.67 roubles monthly, the wages of the tenant being 200 roubles. The government tax was 2 roubles, trade-union dues 4 roubles, contribution to the party funds 4 roubles a month, and subscription to government loans 15 roubles monthly. A trade union, so we were informed, is an organization for the improvement of the economic and cultural conditions of the workers in a particular occupation. It submits criticisms and suggestions for the consideration of the government. In another single room 5 people lived, paying a rent of 26 roubles out of a combined monthly wage of 260 roubles.

We visited a coarse and vulgar "museum of abortion" for the education of the workers. It was like a village peep-show, designed to make the populace shudder. One particular poster and diagram, with an imperial crown at the top, explained how, in Tsarist days, abortion was a crime, liable to a punishment of three years' imprisonment and sometimes to the death penalty (a picture is shown of a woman being hanged), whereas under the present Soviet régime abortion is a minor and harmless operation, comparable to the extraction of a tooth.

The Museum of the Revolution was another tawdry propagandist affair, mostly made up of portraits of prominent revolutionists, an unsavoury-looking lot, together with pictures representing imperialist troops shooting down unarmed workers.

The Second Soviet Hospital of Rostoff is by far the best and most sumptuously equipped post-war hospital we have yet seen in Russia. It was opened only three years ago. It has 1,200 beds, arranged in fine pavilions in a large park. Casual accidents are not admitted, but taken to another hospital. Nearly every department of medicine and surgery is installed, except that there is no special abortorium and no infectious cases. In addition there is a crêche for 40 children who are not ill. The children's pavilion is specially noteworthy. It contains 88 children's cots with 56 beds for the mothers. Most of the pavilion is divided up into large bright cubicles, each with a cot for the patient and a bed for its mother. The walls are of glass, there being two panes of glass to each panel, separated by a half-inch air space, to prevent diffusion of noise. The mother stays in the cubicle with her child and helps in the nursing and attendance. There are also a few ordinary wards for groups of children without their mothers. Most of the wards contain only two or three beds, rarely as many as ten. The mothers, whilst staying in hospital with their children, receive full pay from their factory. There is an excellent maternity ward. Each child at birth is marked with a number in indelible pencil on the forehead, also on a cotton wristlet. The mother's forehead is similarly marked. There are surgical, gynaecological, neurological, and general medical blocks, together with clinical and histological laboratories and a pathological department. There are spacious therapeutic departments for electrical, radiological, balneological, and massage treatment. Each adult ward, never containing more than ten beds, has a special dining-room for those patients who are able to be out of bed. Meals are cooked in a special building, away from the pavilions, and are sent over as required. On all the walls of the waiting-rooms there are health propaganda posters, referring to soap, flies, etc. For these 1,200 beds there is a staff of 91 doctors and two non-medical directors. The senior director is an old gentleman without medical experience "who can read and write and do accounts." His present post is a reward for his faithful communistic services during the Revolution: the doctors tell us that he never interferes in medical matters. Of the 91 doctors, only the 6 juniors are professed communists; the remainder do not interest themselves in communism; they acquiesce in the present régime, but take no active part in politics. The junior members of the medical staff live in the hospital itself; the others attend daily for 5½ hours. The salaries of these medical officers vary from 170 up to 400 roubles per month. Most doctors supplement their income by undertaking an additional billet at some clinic or institute elsewhere. In this way the chief surgeon, who showed us round, makes altogether 500 roubles per month. For the two rooms in which he lives, he pays 21 roubles, also 2 per cent for his trade union, and 1 per cent as government tax, whilst 20 roubles a month are expected towards government loans. He buys his food-rations at government prices. His wife earns 200 roubles in addition.

Private practice is practically non-existent, except in university towns, as above explained.

Any extra food or clothing outside the official allowance costs 4 or 5 times as much as when bought according to ration. A suit of cheap ready-made clothes costs 100 to 120 roubles; boots cost 40 roubles. The children of medical men pay preferential reduced rates of school-fees, about 10 to 15 roubles per annum.

Young doctors, on graduation, are posted by the government to districts where they are most needed. Specially promising men, however, who are recommended by their professors, may undergo additional training, consisting of two years' intensive study followed by two years in general practice, after which they may return to a special department, first as aspirants and later as assistant professors.

Dr. P., the senior surgeon, tells us that the economic position of doctors is admittedly worse since the Revolution, but this is the period of heavy industry development, and the doctors are hoping for better times, some day.

September 4th

Last night, unfortunately for us, there was no "soft" railway coach available on the train from Rostoff to Kharkoff, so we had to choose between waiting 24 hours or travelling "hard" all night and during part of the next day. This we did, perched on a flat board, six feet off the floor, with swarms of men, women, and children pullulating around us. The atmosphere was horrible, but after a few minutes we became acclimatized. The chief drawback was the cimmerian gloom. Every window illuminating the top deck was obscured by a sleeping body.

KHARKOFF, the capital of the Ukraine Republic, is a great busy, booming city. Since the revolution its population has risen from less than 200,000 to over 800,000. The whole place radiates energy; new factories, new workers' villages, new amusement-parks, hospitals, and so on.

The modern quarter of Kharkoff, formerly waste

ground, now has wide boulevards with fine new buildings. At one end of its enormous circular "place," named after Djerjinsky, stands the huge House of Industry, twelve storeys high, built on both sides of a broad street with a couple of galleries spanning the street at the level of the sixth storey. We went by lift to the twelfth storey and thence climbed a couple of flights higher, to get a bird's-eye view of the city.

The former school for daughters of the nobility is now the Marx–Lenin academy. The present Club of the Old Bolsheviks of 1905 is housed in the pre-revolutionary mansion, formerly the town house of an editor named Jussopóvitch. Many large pre-war buildings throughout the town are having a couple of extra storeys added, to give additional accommodation. There is a magnificent new sports stadium, with seats for 12,000 spectators and extra fields for physical culture of various sorts, the whole of them laid out in beautiful flowering gardens. When driving past one of the factories, a small funeral procession emerged through the gates. In front walked a woman, carrying the coffin-lid, then came the corpse in an open coffin, covered with muslin and decorated with bunches of red flowers. Finally walked a group of a dozen women mourners, weeping bitterly. No man was in the party.

We visited a fine new polyclinic, one of ten for the ten districts of Kharkoff. In addition to these, there are twelve Red Cross clinics in the town, doing the same sort of work as the polyclinics, but charging the workers a rouble. The polyclinics are free; consequently patients have to wait a long time before their turn for examination comes; those who are pressed for time patronize a Red Cross clinic. There are also thirty ambulatoria or travelling dispensaries in the town, dealing with surgical, gynaecological, and internal medical ailments.

The polyclinic is an airy, semicircular, two-storey building with consulting-rooms for all classes of illness. These rooms open off its convex side, whilst in the concavity are laboratories and therapeutic rooms, dental, balneological, massage, and electro-therapeutic departments. There is a large lecture-hall seating 300 people. The polyclinic has no beds, but every day 1,500 out-patients are treated, rising to 2,000 in winter-time. Patients who are seriously ill are sent on to a suitable hospital. The medical staff consists of 154 doctors, 70 per cent of whom are women, working in shifts, night and day. Each polyclinic doctor does 2 hours' work in the institute and 2½ hours' visiting in the district or at the various factories. The average monthly wage for a polyclinic doctor is 225 roubles. Many of them, as usual, undertake extra posts whereby they may attain to 500 or even 600 roubles a month.

A huge new tractor-factory with its satellite village, collective-farm markets, etc., has recently been completed. Part of the rough work of this building was done by volunteers from other factories, who gave up their day of rest to help in loading bricks, etc. Our woman guide had been one of them. This factory now employs 10,000 skilled workers, 600 technicians, and about 20,000 unskilled workers and dependents. Its output of tractors is expected to be 50,000 a year.

September 5th

Another long night-journey, lasting up till midday, took us across the wide Ukrainian plains. We were much more comfortable than the previous night, for we were once more travelling "soft," as originally promised. We saw not a single tractor in the harvest fields, although there were numerous men and women using homely scythes and horse-drawn harrows.

KIEFF is the most beautifully situated city we have yet seen. Built on high sandy cliffs overlooking the broad Dnieper, its ups and downs, its golden minarets and church towers, its parks and palaces, are all different from other towns we have visited. We visited the wonderful old Lavra monastery, dating back to the tenth century. Since 1929 its monks have been dispossessed, and it is now transformed into an anti-religious propagandist institution. The cause of their ultimate expulsion was a notorious murder trial, in which one of the monks was convicted of murdering his mistress and dismembering her with an axe. This crime excited the wrath of the populace to such a pitch that all the other

PLAYERS WITH THE CRUCIFIX

On the blade: Armed Aggression against the U.S.S.R.

600 monks were thrown out of the monastery. Just outside the boundary of the Lavra itself is the curious twelfth-century church of *Spass-na-Berestol* (the Saviour in Berestol) with its six green cupolas. It is built of alternate rows of stone blocks and curious flat bricks, numbers of which are arranged in the outer walls so as to form a bas-relief of crosses, sometimes with one, sometimes with two cross-bars. Other bricks are arranged in a swastika pattern, close beneath the gable, so-called *meandres*. We enter the Lavra monastery through a twelfth-century gateway surmounted by a small church. Inside the walled rampart is a huge four-storey pillared campanile, surmounted by a golden dome. To reach the open space in which the bell-tower stands, we pass along a street of little white one-storey houses, formerly the private dwellings of the archimandrites. The Uspensky cathedral (Cathedral of the Assumption) is built around a still older eleventh-century church. It is resplendent with gold furniture and decorations. The golden crucifix over the entrance gateway now flies the red flag. Inside the cathedral are sumptuous golden plates and ornaments presented by successive Russian emperors. There is a huge embossed silver-gilt altar, the gift of the Empress Elizabeth, also magnificent large golden ikons and gilded pillars and walls. The mummified body of the sainted Metropolitan Tobolski, dating from 1780, is shown in a glass-covered coffin. One of the three skulls of St. Vladimir who first christianized Russia in the tenth

century is here shown. (Two other skulls in different collections of relics are also claimed as authentic.) Also the famous dark Madonna of the fourteenth century—a lovely face with wistful eyes, mounted in golden coverings with large jewels affixed. Several cabinets and coffin-lids are specially constructed for the collection of holy relics. One coffin-lid has 88 little hollow panels, each labelled with a description of a relic.

The death-mask of Stolypin, who was assassinated in the opera-house of Kieff in 1911, is also seen. His body is buried just outside the cathedral, under a magnificent marble slab and cross. There is a silver-gilt coffin of St. Theodosius, the founder of this monastery, whose chilly cell we inspected later in the catacombs below. In one of the walls of the cathedral is a beautiful sixteenth-century red marble monument, showing a semi-recumbent warrior, Prince Ostrovsky, lying in a deep recess overhung by a graceful stone curtain. Until a few weeks ago the red marble had been hidden beneath numerous coats of blue paint; these have only recently been chipped off.

The Lavra catacombs, excavated in the cliffs overlooking the river, are approached through a gloomy wooden tunnel, vaulted on its roof and lit along one side only, through an open space interrupted by a series of little wooden pillars. The catacombs themselves have the usual chilly winding passages, flanked by coffins all the way. Some of these have glass lids, to display the mummified remains within, clad in handsome vestments. There are also three small underground chapels and a special repairing-room, or beauty-parlour, for the restoration and embellishment of saintly mummies.

The Fourth Psycho-Neurological Institute of 200 beds (sometimes increased to 250) has four divisions, for vegetative diseases, organic diseases, neuroses, and psycho-neuroses respectively. There are clinical and pathological laboratories, a morbid anatomy department (post-mortem examinations are obligatory), and elaborately equipped electrical and balneological departments. There is also a polyclinic for nervous maladies. Incurable or chronic patients in this and other hospitals are kept for 1½ months, after which they either go home on a 40 per cent pension or are sent to special institutions for chronic cases. There are 40 doctors, half of whom are women. Professor Mankovski is the chief of the organic department, and his assistant, Dr. Mintz, who showed us round, demonstrated a number of interesting cases in the wards. These specialist doctors receive 250 roubles a month, whilst the professor gets 300 roubles. He also has a considerable private consulting practice, which may bring his monthly income up to 1,500 roubles. The doctors are apparently resigned to the meagreness of these emoluments. They hope for better things in future, when the present industrial effort is over.

We attended a popular cinema show this evening in Kieff. There was a crowded audience, with a large proportion of Red Army soldiers. The pictures illustrated the iniquity of the kulaks or private farmers, hiding grain from the Government and stirring up counter-revolution against the benevolent communist party. Then there was a series of topical pictures showing the anniversary demonstrations held this very day in celebration of the Young Communist party. The leading orators were filmed, haranguing the crowd. I never saw a more degraded or malignant type of faces—almost bestial—than in these orators. Such films would be excellent anti-communist propaganda for exhibition before an ordinary civilized audience.

September 6th

The cathedral of St. Sofia in Kieff, built by Prince Yaroslav the Wise in the eleventh century, is approached through a square seventeenth-century campanile of four storeys with a gilded dome. The imperial double-headed Russian eagle still adorns its base.

Like the church of Spass-na-Berestol, this cathedral is built of alternate layers of stone blocks and narrow flat bricks. The cathedral is still in use for worship. In the vestibule we met the bishop himself, a quiet, refined man in lay garments with a short pointed beard. We bade our interpreter tell him how we appreciated the honour of meeting him.

He said things were "rather hard," but did not tell us more. We judged it discreet to leave it at that.

The cathedral itself has wonderful mosaics under its dome and along the aisles, as bright to-day as when they were executed by Byzantine artists nine hundred years ago. There are the usual heavy silver-gilt ikons, altar furniture, etc. Also some curious old frescoes illustrating non-religious subjects, such as hunting scenes. We were shown a sixth-century carved coffin of white marble, brought from Byzantium for the tomb of Prince Yaroslav. This had been thrown into the river by barbarian Turks many centuries ago, but was subsequently recovered and brought back, empty, of course, to the old cathedral. Our guide says that a commission of archaeologists is again fishing in the river to try to find the lid.

September 7th

Last night we crossed the Russo–Polish frontier. The Customs-house examinations, both Russian and Polish, were tedious, but not severe. We were not allowed to bring any Russian roubles out of the country. Fortunately we had spent all our roubles except for one-and-a-half between us. These were just enough to tip the baggage-porter.

The moment one crosses the frontier, on the way to Warsaw, the differences between the two peoples and countries are at once evident. Here in Poland the houses, farms, and factories are spick and span, the window-panes are polished, the posts and railings are painted. The Pole is smartly dressed, alert, courteous, and independent. Officers salute when talking to us. The whole people, in spite of their post-war troubles, look happy and busy. The working men are totally unlike the Soviet "mass-man" in dress and bearing. The Soviet "comrade," shabby and grubby, seems unused to individualistic life, which seems to cow him, unless he can sustain his confidence by reciting communistic catch phrases about the "dictatorship of the proletariat," the "stamping out of exploiters" who hire exploitees, and so on. He is at his happiest when moving obediently in a procession behind a brass band, in a forest of red banners and flags.

In WARSAW we secured an English-speaking guide and spent a busy day seeing the ordinary tourist sights. The Royal Palace on the bank of the broad Vistula contains a number of interesting historical relics, including the heart of Kosciusko, the great Polish patriot (1746–1817), preserved in the Palace Chapel. Many of the best pictures and articles of furniture were looted by the Russians during the war, but under the terms of a recent treaty some of these have been restored to their original places, and more are being received month by month. Opposite the royal palace in the public square is the monument to Sigismund III, a tall figure on top of a high column.

Warsaw, out of a population of about 1,200,000,

contains some 500,000 Jews. The old-fashioned Jewish quarter is interesting but sordid, thronged by ancient bearded patriarchs with long ringlets, by Jewesses with wigs (the sign of a married woman), and by a few Gentiles. We saw two women thieves being marched to gaol between a couple of gendarmes with a small procession of twenty or thirty friends and acquaintances following up, to keep them cheery.

The modern Russian cathedral in Warsaw has a surface which is deep-blue, outside and in. Its inner dome is studded with electrically lighted stars in a blue firmament. We were shown the archiepiscopal robes, ikons, and treasures.

The boulevards are beautifully laid out, reminding one of the Champs-Élysées in Paris. Along one side of the smartest avenue is a whole row of foreign embassies, facing a magnificent public park. In the park is a colossal statue of Chopin, the composer, seated under a tree with spreading golden branches. The Belvedere, formerly the palace of the Russian governor, is where the present Polish dictator, Marshal Pilsudski, now resides.

Later we drove about ten miles out into the country and visited the Willanoff Palace belonging to a Polish nobleman, Count Branitski. It is full of pictures, statuary, and antiques, some of them valuable, others of little interest. We also saw the chapel in which Sobietski (1659) died.

The whole atmosphere of Warsaw, with its smart

well-groomed streets and well-dressed inhabitants and its general feeling of initiative and energy, was specially bracing after the depressing surroundings of proletariat Russia. We had a good hotel with capital bathrooms and excellent food. Thus refreshed, we embarked on the night train for Berlin.

CHAPTER VI

SOME CONCLUSIONS

SOVIET Russia is neither the heaven of which the Red communist brays so loudly (and all the more confidently if he himself has never been to Russia) nor is it the hell which some die-hard capitalistic journals would have us believe. Rather is it a curious sort of purgatory, with an indescribable joyless atmosphere about it, different from that in any civilized country. This atmosphere begins to make itself felt from the first moment when one steps on board a Soviet ship at London Bridge, and the sailor who eagerly carries one's baggage to the allotted cabin refuses, sadly but firmly, to accept a tip, remarking "*nye pologayet*," i.e. "we don't have that sort of thing."

The visitor travelling in Russia is at first amused, interested, and stimulated; later he becomes bored, and finally nauseated, by the plethora of blood-red cotton banners with their communistic slogans, by the innumerable statues, busts, and pictures of Lenin, and by the ceaseless socialistic and anti-capitalistic propaganda of newspapers, radios, theatrical plays, and cinema films. Every public building and museum, every workers' club, reading-room, and dining-room, every hospital ward, school-room and infants' crêche, is blazoned with communistic maxims and swathed in scarlet flags and banners. The stately pre-war palaces and mansions, now sordid and dilapidated, are, nearly all of them, grotesquely diverted from their original purposes. Churches are now transformed into anti-religious museums, workers' clubs, cinemas, or dancing-halls; schools are occupied by trade-union offices; private villas are partitioned off into workers' dwellings, or used as country rest-homes. The statues of former Tsars have been torn down, and on their pedestals stand the effigies of Lenin or of Marx.

Nevertheless, in striking contrast to these destructive efforts, the honest observer cannot fail to note the feverish activity with which Soviet Russia is erecting huge new factories and blocks of ultra-modern buildings to house her town workers, providing them, moreover, with club-houses, gymnasiums, theatres, and sports grounds. The colossal Dnieperstroi dam, recently completed at enormous outlay, for the production and distribution of electric power throughout the south of Russia, is an achievement which cannot be gainsaid.

Still more impressive is the elaborate organization of her public health services. Some of these are diametrically opposed to the codes of social life in western countries. Others, however, constitute a challenge to capitalist governments, a challenge which they would do well to take up, and, if possible, to surpass.

Prophylactoria for the prevention of bodily diseases; official abortoria for those women who desire to avoid motherhood; lavishly equipped maternity institutes for mothers who decide to have children; crêches for infants, polyclinics for the treatment of early and minor maladies; hospitals, infirmaries, and convalescent homes for persons who require more serious treatment (many of them dating from pre-Soviet days); night homes for tuberculous town-workers still able to go to work in the day-time; rest-homes where workers can spend their official holidays: these and similar institutions are all provided by the State, free of cost. The only economy in Russian public health administration seems to be the meagre wages meted out to the medical officers in charge of these institutions. Their standard rate of pay is 250 roubles a month, less than that of the skilled factory hand, and much less than that of the technician and even of certain special manual workers who may receive as much as 700 roubles a month.

The value of the rouble, moreover, is entirely fictitious. No roubles may be taken out of Russia. The foreign expert who has been lured into the country and paid a handsome salary, in roubles, finds that he cannot exchange his savings for foreign valuta, but must hand over everything at the frontier. Thrift is discountenanced and the worker is encouraged to spend his last kopeck, knowing that if he dies possessed of any savings they will only be appropriated by the State, since no one may execute a will in Russia nowadays.

Marriage and divorce are dealt out by a young woman clerk, seated at an office table, with a book of marriage registrations at one side and a divorce volume at the other.

Other Soviet institutions may perhaps seem Utopian, but they compel us furiously to think. Take, for example, their penal system. Counter-revolutionary activities are sternly dealt with, either by the death penalty or by transportation, under conditions of unspeakable cruelty, to distant prison camps in the northern forests. On the other hand, ordinary criminals, such as murderers, embezzlers, and burglars, are detained in comfortable institutions, amazingly different from prisons in other countries. In such institutions there is no solitary confinement, nor are the prisoners withdrawn from social intercourse with their fellow-inmates. Remunerative work, education, daily amusements, and recreations are provided, and the indoor warders are elected by the prisoners themselves. No wonder that no inmate tries to escape from such a home, especially when we bear in mind the dreary level of discomfort in which the average Russian citizen exists.

Being neither a politician nor a political economist, I am not competent to discuss the merits of the famous Five-Year Plan devised by the Soviet government for the establishment of its heavy manufacturing industries, for the urbanization of the peasant workers, and for the collectivization of agriculture. Nevertheless I have made careful inquiries, not only by personal observations, but also by additional information obtained from expert engineers, agriculturists, and business men. The weight of evidence seems to show that, in some respects, the Five-Year Plan has been a partial success; in others a conspicuous failure. Thus, for example, great factories have been erected in various cities and equipped with the best and latest machinery imported from abroad. These factories ostensibly turn out by mass-production large numbers of automobiles, tractors, railway rolling-stock, etc. One great automobile factory which we visited and carefully inspected, in company with a distinguished English engineer, possessed the full equipment and personnel requisite for the turning out of motor-cars standardized by mass-production. The completed cars, however, when delivered at the end of the moving belt, were devoid both of radiators and magnetos; these were being made, so we were told, in another government factory, hundreds of miles away. This, of course, may have been only a temporary hold-up, but it gives an interesting indication of the standard of efficiency of some of these great new ventures. Whilst on the subject of tractors and "combines," designed for use in the government "collective" farms, these machines are doubtless being manufactured in considerable numbers, as claimed by the Soviet government. But in a two days' railway journey across the great Ukrainian plain during harvest-time, a careful look-out failed to observe a single tractor or "combine" on the fields. The crops were still being mown by hand-scythes and the ground was being harrowed by horse-drawn harrows. The output of grain, as computed by independent experts over a period of several months, is far below the figures claimed by the Government statistics. A certain amount of privation as regards food-stuffs, therefore, seems inevitable. The workers, however, are encouraged to put up with these hardships, buoyed by the hope of the successful Five-Year Plan and of the promised communistic millennium which is to follow.

The increasing output of heavy industries is invariably misrepresented in the propagandist museums as a steep, ever-rising curve, without even a temporary downward deflection. How far this is from the truth is shown in a recent article by Molotoff himself,[1] chairman of the Council of Commissars. He complains of the lack of personal responsibility on the part of the workers with regard to the machinery and mechanisms confided to their charge. He even admits that the equalization of wages of manual and technical workers, according to communistic principles, has led to a blunting of interest on the part of the skilled workers, of whom there is a scarcity, so that he now foresees the necessity for readmitting the heretical expedient of increased pay for better work. This may prove the thin end

[1] *Voks*, 1932. No. 1. pp. 14–47.

of the wedge, by creating a petty bourgeoisie. Molotoff also complains of the imperfect organization of the collective farms under the present arrangement whereby equal payment is made to all workers, whether skilled or unskilled, industrious or idle. And yet, in spite of this, it is curious how obstinately he insists on the necessity for the ultimate elimination of the private farmer or "kulak," and the driving of all private farmers into the collective farms.

In a further discussion of the heavy industries problem, Kuibyshev,[1] chairman of the State Planning Committee of the S.S.S.R., complains bitterly not only of the actual diminution during 1931 of coal production and the falling off in railway transport, but also of the lowered output of iron and steel. To quote his own words: "We are wasting atrociously both fuel and metal, of which we are already short; finally, the bad quality of goods which are produced is also a waste of national economic resources."

In the face of admissions like these, the misleading curves and inflated statistics in the Soviet journals cannot be regarded as even approximately accurate; they are evidently devised for crude consumption, being pious hopes of what the communistic party would wish, but have failed, to achieve.

When we come to the subject of the educational

[1] *Voks*, 1932. No. 1. pp. 48–76.

programme, the liquidation of illiteracy in some parts of Soviet Russia is certainly advancing steadily. For this we must give her credit. But, simultaneously with this educational progress, iron shutters are clamped over the windows of the student's mind, so that no illumination save the red light of communistic doctrine is allowed to enter. Freedom of speech is sternly repressed. Freedom of thought cannot be extinguished even by a communist government. The existence of a Supreme Being is officially derided. No religious instruction (apart from the veneration of Lenin, and to a lesser extent of Marx) may be taught to anyone below the age of eighteen. Parental discipline is a thing of the past. Youth no longer pays regard to the wisdom or experience of maturity. All anti-communistic publications are forbidden. Whatever pronouncement happens to be the opinion of a numerical majority of the communist ruling party at the moment is imposed on the remaining 98 per cent of the population, as a decree from which there is no appeal. The people are constantly and noisily assured that they are being governed by a "dictatorship of the proletariat," which is an obvious and glaring untruth.

With regard to the general social atmosphere of Soviet Russia, it must be realized by every thinking Russian (although in Russia he does not dare to say so) that the small communist party exercises a crushing tyranny over a sullen and cowed population. The old aristocracy, the pre-war intelligentsia, the capitalist and the bourgeois class with its private enterprise, having all been exterminated, Russian citizens are now reduced to a condition of terrorism and slavery dominated by a ruthless and fanatical despotism, labelled as democracy. How long the intelligence of the rising generation of Russians will tolerate this twilight training remains to be seen.

Soviet Russia is breeding a new species of anthropoid, the "mass-man" or *homo proletarius* differing in many respects from the *homo sapiens* of other countries. But sooner or later younger Russians are bound to realize the insecurity of the basis on which the present organization is founded. The communists may then find that they have raised a Frankenstein which will turn and rend them.

It is obvious, in any case, that social conditions in Russia have not attained to final stability. Whether the country is heading for prosperity or disaster, time alone will tell.

INDEX

9781138083653.